FREEDOM *from* ADDICTION

DAVID SIMON, M.D.
DEEPAK CHOPRA, M.D.

*F*REEDOM
from
*A*DDICTION

The CHOPRA CENTER *Method for*
Overcoming Destructive Habits

Health Communications, Inc.
Deerfield Beach, Florida

www.hcibooks.com

Library of Congress Cataloging-in-Publication Data

Simon, David.

Freedom from addiction : the Chopra Center method for overcoming destructive habits / David Simon & Deepak Chopra.

p. cm.

Includes bibliographical references and index.

ISBN-13: 978-0-7573-0578-8 (trade paper)

ISBN-10: 0-7573-0578-4 (trade paper)

1. Substance abuse—Prevention. 2. Self-actualization (Psychology) 3. Healing. 4. Mental healing. 5. Spiritual healing. 6. Emotional maturity. I. Chopra, Deepak. II. Chopra Center for Wellbeing. III. Title.

HV4998.S56 2008

616.86'06—dc22

2007012741

©2007 David Simon and Deepak Chopra

Publisher: Health Communications, Inc.
3201 S.W. 15th Street
Deerfield Beach, FL 33442-8190

Cover design by Larissa Hise Henoch
Inside book design by Dawn Von Strolley Grove

Contents

Introduction

"I ACCEPT THAT I AM an alcoholic," Dan confessed, "but I just can't handle going to A.A. meetings. I feel more depressed than inspired by everyone's stories, and I don't like the idea that the central focus for the rest of my life has to be defining myself as powerless."

Although Dan had been sober for over three years, he felt the need to see his drinking problem in a new light. He wanted to see if he could redefine himself in a way that allowed for personal growth.

We live on a planet that offers many potential addictions. As a human being, you have almost certainly engaged in a habit that seemed to call to you, even though it had undesirable side effects. People have a great capacity to participate in behaviors that provide momentary pleasure only to extract an emotional or physical toll. Although relatively few of us inject heroin or smoke crack cocaine, many among us overeat, overdrink, overthink, smoke cigarettes, compulsively buy things we do not need, gamble away our hard-earned money, and otherwise make choices that do not nourish our bodies, minds, or souls.

Indeed, addiction is the most widespread problem in our society. The emotional and physical pain experienced by people with addictions and their families is incalculable. The direct and indirect economic costs of addiction exceed hundreds of billions of dollars worldwide. Yet we are losing the "war on drugs" because we have failed to recognize that the enemy is a hidden aspect of ourselves, a subconscious drive to sacrifice long-term peace for short-term relief. This book is our effort to reframe the conflict surrounding addiction and expand your opportunities for lasting peace.

What's New in Recovery?

Over the past seventy years, millions of people seeking to overcome addictive behaviors have embarked on a Twelve-Step program. First introduced as the basic tenets of Alcoholics Anonymous (A.A.), the Twelve Steps have been adopted by many other support groups, including, but not limited to, Narcotics Anonymous, Cocaine Anonymous, Overeaters Anonymous, Gamblers Anonymous, Sexaholics Anonymous, Debtors Anonymous, Eating Disorders Anonymous, and Workaholics Anonymous. For those who can embrace the basic principles and appreciate the community of others waging their own battles against personal demons, Twelve-Step programs provide valuable support.

The Twelve Steps are not for everyone, however. For some, the religious overtones are incompatible with their core personal beliefs, while for others, the Twelve Steps are not religious enough. The most common reason we hear at the Chopra Center for why people do not resonate with A.A. is its emphasis on personal powerlessness. Most secular and religious philosophies highlight the principle that we are responsible for our choices in life. The first step in Twelve-Step programs requires an admission of powerlessness that some people are not able or willing to embrace. The implication that people with bad habits must consider themselves lifelong victims of an incurable condition is, for some, untenable. For those who believe free will is a distinguishing feature of human beings, admitting that one has lost free will stops the recovery process before it begins.

The Twelve-Step response to this criticism is that addicts have lost the ability to freely choose because they are so impaired by their addiction. Recognizing this, the first step requires an admission that the addict is powerless over the addiction, while the second step requires embracing the belief that a greater power is required to restore sanity.

We think it's possible to reconcile the opposing viewpoints of choice versus powerlessness. The Chopra Center philosophy and approach to addiction highlights the paradox that every life seeks to resolve—the apparent conflict between our individuality and our universality.

The Paradox of Individuality Versus Universality

Life can be challenging, and there are times when we feel compelled to alleviate the distress quickly. Behaviors that temporarily anesthetize the pain and anxiety of loss, disappointment, separation, alienation, frustration, or loneliness can develop into habits and addictions that trade short-term relief for longer-term distress. This natural impulse to do or take whatever is necessary to relieve the distress is the basis of addiction. Our goal is to offer you better alternatives to coping with life's challenges and disappointments.

As individuals we all have specific intentions and desires, which we strive to manifest through our choices and actions. We develop habits of behavior in our quest to satisfy our needs for security, self-esteem, sensory gratification, power, and material acquisition. These are the needs of our individuality, which we try to fill with things outside of ourselves. And yet, at another level, we recognize that our emptiness inside cannot be filled from outside. Our compulsion to acquire, attain, accomplish, and achieve will not lead to lasting peace or inner satisfaction. A spiritual life seeks to integrate the quest to fulfill our individual needs through the power of intention with an internal state of peace and contentment generated through the power of surrender. Knowing when to exercise will and when to accept things as they are requires skill and finesse.

Changing Habits with the Chopra Center Perspective

If you drive down the same dirt road day after day, your car will form ruts in the road that will limit your ability to maneuver. Unless you pay attention and become mindful, your car will default to the ruts, and in doing so, reinforce the prior patterns in the dirt. If you want to get out of the rut, you will need to consciously choose another path and reinforce this new path until it becomes your established way of traveling. Similarly, the principles in this book offer a new path to travel—a path to freedom.

Of course, not all habits are harmful. Exercising regularly, eating healthy foods, playing music, doing yoga, meditating, working in the garden, flossing your teeth, and communicating consciously are habits that can be cultivated and generate positive side effects. Some habits have life-affirming consequences, and some have life-damaging ones. Our challenge is to identify potentially destructive habits, understand the needs they serve, make the conscious decision to release them, and then replace them with healthier choices. We would like to convince you to trade your potentially destructive habits for those that celebrate life.

We have been exploring the relationship between body, mind, and spirit for more than thirty years. The Chopra Center, founded over a decade ago, provides a place where healing and transformation are fostered. We care for people in the midst of physical, emotional, and spiritual crises. We know the suffering that people can experience in life and the power of the human soul to awaken innate recuperative powers.

We also know how often our misery is the result of choices we make. People engage repeatedly in patterns of behavior that consciously or unconsciously lead to suffering. Human beings are remarkably creative in their ability to deny the negative consequences of the compulsions that drive them. In fact, this talent for denial is widespread.

The Chopra Center was founded on the belief that we share an underlying unity that transcends our diversity. Each of us is an expression of the same creative intelligence that pervades all form and phenomena. When we lose our connection to this unity, the result is emotional or physical distress. Health is regained when we return to wholeness. The human experience is a game of hide-and-seek, in which we lose ourselves at times to rediscover ourselves. Our role at the Chopra Center is to help people remove the shrouds that obscure their intrinsic wholeness—their essential holiness. Through this rediscovery we help people become capable of making choices that are in alignment with their higher purpose.

Unhealthy habits create suffering, and yet there are times when life seems too painful to face directly, and therefore shortcuts to relief are almost irresistible. Unfortunately, it is often the case that the more rapid the relief, the shorter the reprieve. The shorter the reprieve, the easier it is to develop an addiction. The problem with addictions is that they provide diminishing returns with increasing risks—the price escalates for something of diminishing value. We cannot, however, expect people to "just say no." We need to recognize the needs that drive people's addictions and offer creative options to satisfy them.

It can be argued that there is something inherent in the human soul that seeks a shift in perspective. The English novelist Aldous Huxley wrote, "Always and everywhere, human beings have felt the radical inadequacy of being their insulated selves and not something else, something wider, something in the Wordsworthian phrase, 'far more deeply interfused.' To go beyond the insulated self is such a liberation that, even when self-transcendence is through nausea into frenzy, through cramps into hallucinations and coma, the drug-induced experience has been regarded by primitives and even by the highly civilized as intrinsically divine."[1]

The quest to expand our sense of self is a core human impulse, and yet, a temporary altering of boundaries only to return to a more constricted state provides limited benefits. A genuine transformation in identity requires practice and knowledge. To release life-constricting habits and replace them with life-expanding ones requires attention and intention. We encourage you to commit to this process to shed your old habits and create a fresh start.

Modulating from Without

Addictions serve a purpose. When people seek a shift in their emotional state and do not know how to create the change from within, they reach for something outside. Psychoactive chemicals can change one's mood or emotion, but only temporarily. When the drug is gone, the discontent, discomfort, or distress is often worse than before. Then the person must choose either to seek a more lasting shift or re-engage in another short-term dose of relief.

Alcohol and drugs consume tremendous resources. Used judiciously, they can add unique flavors to life, but misused they wreak havoc on individuals, families, and communities. For centuries, societies have attempted to reduce the potential harm addictive behaviors can cause.

The adage, "The more things change, the more they stay the same," aptly applies to addiction therapy. The history of addiction treatment is characterized by enthusiasm for a particular approach more than by any objective validation of outcome. A unifying theory and generally accepted therapeutic approach have been elusive. Now, as in times past, forces promoting the criminalization of addiction clash with those convinced it should be viewed biologically and treated as an illness. This is a critical argument because about a third of current federal inmates are serving time for drug-related offenses, while the "war on drugs" costs our society more than $50 billion each year.

Although efforts to find the underlying biological or genetic factors explaining alcoholism and drug addiction have yielded some fruits, it's clear that hereditary and biochemical contributions are complex and variable. Most experts no longer believe we will find a simple genetic explanation for addiction or a silver bullet to vanquish the demons.

Despite these challenges, we believe that people can re-create themselves. We have seen how motivated people can cast off a familiar but outmoded sense of self to embrace a more expanded perspective. A new perspective enables a new thought process and a new physiology to emerge. Human beings are capable of learning new tricks.

Core Needs and Beliefs

If you are reading these words because you suspect you have a life-harming addiction, the first compulsion we want you to release is self-disdain. In terms of core needs, people with addictions are no different than other people. The primary distinction is that they have chosen a socially unacceptable or biologically undesirable way to meet their needs. Do not add insult to injury by wasting time or energy denigrating yourself over your addiction. Instead let's use that energy for healing and transformation.

Life is for learning. The knowledge we acquire helps us fulfill our needs and desires, whether they are material, physical, emotional, or spiritual. If we find ourselves in a situation that creates distress for ourselves or others, it's usually a signal that we need to learn something new. This may be understanding something for the first time, or replacing a misunderstanding with more useful knowledge.

Our experience with people struggling with unhealthy habits is that they carry a number of misunderstandings about the nature of their condition. Replacing these false beliefs with useful beliefs begins the journey to healing and transformation.

Please read the authentic beliefs below several times until you see their inherent truth. Once you see their legitimacy, memorize them.

- I am doing my best given my current psychological and spiritual resources.
- I have no desire to hurt anyone, including myself, as a consequence of my addiction.
- Although I am good at rationalizing my addiction, I know at the core of my being that my habit is not serving my body, mind, or soul.
- I recognize at some level that my addiction is a substitute for love.
- I would free myself of this life-damaging habit if I could find a life-honoring substitute of equal or greater efficacy.
- Although at times I may doubt it, I know at the deepest level of my being that I am capable of releasing this negative habit and replacing it with positive ones.
- Seeking relief through substances is an expression of my spiritual quest to find peace.

We are not asking you to turn these statements into affirmations. We are asking you to recognize their inherent truthfulness. Let's review them one by one.

1. I am doing my best given my current psychological and spiritual resources.

This is a core truth of life. We are all doing our best, given our awareness of our needs and our means to meet them. A woman who goes shopping and adds several hundred dollars to an already overextended credit card account is engaging in a compulsive behavior because she cannot think of another way to soothe her anxiety. A stressed businessman who drinks a fifth of vodka upon arriving at home is doing so because he cannot envision another effective way to calm his agitation.

Expanding awareness of the consequences of our decisions enables us to make more conscious choices. Creativity is suppressed when we can only see things in a limited way. Creativity flows when we are able to view our challenges from a more expanded perspective. We will explore means to expand awareness throughout this book.

2. I have no desire to hurt anyone, including myself, as a consequence of my addiction.

Because addictive behavior has the potential to create great suffering for both addicts and the people around them, it sometimes appears as if there is a destructive intention underlying the behavior. This is not the case. The harmful consequences of addictive behavior are an unwanted side effect of the attempt to relieve the pain of insecurity, loneliness, or unworthiness. If people are able to find alternative sources of relief for their pain, they willingly relinquish the habit that has potentially destructive consequences. Our goal is to help you find acceptable alternatives to your addiction so you will not experience its painful consequences.

3. Although I am good at rationalizing my addiction, I know at the core of my being that my habit is not serving my body, mind, or soul.

The human mind is remarkably adept at justifying behaviors that may not be life supporting. From "I don't need to wear a seat belt because I'm only driving a short distance," to "A half-a-pack per day is not much worse than breathing the air in Los Angeles," we each develop a personal repertoire of psychological defenses to explain away behaviors that do not truly serve us. When we quiet our inner turbulence and relinquish our resistance to facing the truth, we can resolve the arguments we are having with ourselves and align our choices with our higher purpose. We will be offering you ways to calm the mental agitation that allows you to continue deceiving yourself.

4. I recognize at some level that my addiction is a substitute for love.

The opposite of love is separation. When we are feeling connected to something that expands our sense of self, we feel secure, comfortable, and balanced. When we do not have safe and nurturing associations, we experience anxiety, hostility, and depression. Addictive behaviors and substances are poor substitutions for the love that flows in nourishing relationships. Learning to heal our core relationships and cultivate skills in conscious communication can provide the inner peace that eliminates the need for self-medication.

5. I would free myself of this life-damaging habit if I could find a life-honoring substitute of equal or greater efficacy.

A person will refuse to give up a dilapidated car because he has no alternative means of transportation—until you offer him a newer model in good running condition. We cannot expect people to relinquish toxic behaviors that provide some relief without offering something to replace them. Throughout this book we'll be suggesting nourishing alternatives that can substitute for life-harming habits. Although they may not offer the dramatic or instantaneous relief of an addictive behavior, they support evolutionary personal development and self-generated ecstasy.

6. Although at times I may doubt it, I know at the deepest level of my being that I am capable of releasing this negative habit and replacing it with positive ones.

Many people suffering with addictions genuinely doubt that they possess the inner resources to heal. During our years of practicing medicine, we've seen that people who are not ready to change will not. Fortunately we've also seen that when people are clear that they want a new life, nothing stands in their way of creating it.

If now is the time you are willing to commit to healing and transformation, you already have within you the capacity to manifest the life you want. The mechanics to fulfill a desire are inherent in the intention. The fact that you are reading these words implies that at some level of your being, you can already envision the change you want to manifest.

7. Seeking relief through substances is an expression of my essential spiritual nature.

The goal of every behavior is comfort and inner peace. Whether you seek comfort through meditation, hugging your spouse, smoking a cigarette, or drinking martinis, the intention is the same. We engage in behaviors that relieve anxiety and help us feel more comfortable within ourselves.

People with addictive behaviors are often intensely aware of the irreconcilable paradoxes of life, and they therefore feel existential pain most acutely. Our goal is to help you redirect your desire from finding relief through a life-harming behavior to finding peace through a life-celebrating spiritual practice.

Our life energy is precious. When we direct it consciously,

we are able to manifest our deepest intentions for creativity and freedom. Through our daily work with guests at the Chopra Center for Wellbeing, we have become convinced that when people are ready to exchange their energy-wasting habits for those that enliven their essential vitality, healing and transformation become irresistible.

Envisioning Freedom from Your Addiction

DEBORAH WAS GOING THROUGH *a rough year. Her mother had recently passed away after a long illness, and shortly thereafter, her husband announced he was leaving her. Just as her life seemed to be falling apart, she was rear-ended while stopped at a traffic light, resulting in a whiplash injury.*

Although her imaging studies showed only mild degenerative changes, her neck pain was incapacitating. After trials of other medications, she was prescribed Vicodin by her family doctor. She liked the analgesic effect on her neck and emotional pain. Within a short time, she was taking

more than twelve tablets per day, and was requesting pre-
scriptions from three different doctors.

She recognized she had a problem when she went three
days without moving her bowels and was spending more
time thinking about how she could replenish her supply
than the underlying pain she was initially treating.

An ancient expression in the Yoga tradition proclaims, "I am not in the world; the world is in me." Although at first glance this bold statement may come across as narcissistic, we see it as a clear expression of human reality. At every moment of life, there are uncountable events occurring simultaneously. As you are reading these words, there are people being born while others are dying. There are people making love while others are heatedly arguing. One person is getting a promotion; another is being fired. Someone is starting a new business; another person is declaring bankruptcy. Some are feasting while others are starving. An unfathomable multitude of possible experiences are unfolding at every moment; still, each of us focuses on our particular concerns while filtering out the others.

Think of it this way: If you are hiking up a wooded mountainside, there will be times when you cannot see the peak. Still, you carry the inner map of where you've been, where you are, and where you want to go. This inner map of your world enables you to navigate in pursuit of your goals. As a result of your inner atlas, you selectively focus on those external markers that reinforce your worldview and filter out those that do not.

Where is this process of selective attention and intention occurring? The answer is in consciousness. As we ingest the raw sensory material of the world, sounds, sensations, sights, tastes, and smells are transmitted as trains of energy and information through the neural networks of our nervous system. Somehow, from all of this energy and information, we are able to create a four-dimensional picture of the world that seems real to us. In consciousness we create an outside world that cannot be measured objectively or scientifically, but is very real to us.

Knowing that you co-create your reality is powerful information. It means that you can relinquish the idea that your life is rigidly predetermined and open up to the possibility that whatever has transpired thus far, you have the capacity to create something new. This shift in awareness is the first step toward manifesting your deepest desires for happiness, health, and love.

Once you recognize the possibilities of creating a new reality, it becomes your opportunity and responsibility to envision what it is you'd like to create. Despite the script you've been reading up until this point, you have the capacity to begin writing new dialogues. Assuming authority for your life means accepting the role of author as well as the leading character in your story line.

Listening Within

To assist you in visualizing what you'd like to see unfold in your life, consider the following themes. These are designed to help you go beyond your usual self-dialogue and think authentically about what you want and are capable of creating in your life. To gain the most benefit from this process, we encourage you to review the topic and consider the questions. Then close your eyes; take a few slow, deep breaths; and, centering your awareness in your heart, contemplate the question, listening for insights that enter into consciousness from a deeper place within you.

It is often helpful to record your insights in a journal. The process of documenting your thoughts and feelings helps expand your perspective while catalyzing healing and transformation.

1. What Need Is Your Addiction Filling?

All behaviors are motivated by the desire to increase comfort or decrease pain. Addictive behaviors are driven by the belief that the behavior can fulfill needs that other choices cannot.

Questions for Reflection:
- Can I identify the need my habit is attempting to fulfill?
- Do I believe I can substitute a nourishing habit for a toxic one?

- Do I believe I will need to practice total abstinence from my harmful habit or that I can manage my habit to reduce the harm it is causing?

2. Is Addiction a Disease or a Choice?

A perennial question in the addiction field is whether addictive behavior is an illness that can be treated as a chronic medical condition or a conditioned behavior that can be changed through intention and will.

Questions for Reflection:

- Do I believe I have a disease over which I have no control, or do I believe I have some control over my habit?
- Am I experiencing negative consequences because of my choices, or do I think I am managing well enough?
- Am I prepared to change my thinking, behaviors, and relationships if that will enable me to free myself from my habit?

3. Am I Repeating the Same Behaviors but Expecting a Different Outcome?

Repeated behaviors generate their own self-perpetuation. Getting out of a rut requires conscious, sustained attention.

Questions for Reflection:

- What are the patterns in my life that will continue if I do not consciously change them?

- What changes in my thinking are required for me to change my behaviors?
- What are the ways my habits sabotage my efforts to change direction?

4. What Do I Deserve?

Our core beliefs about whether we deserve to enjoy or suffer in life drive our behaviors. This basic belief is difficult to change, but we must do so if we are to stop making choices that create pain.

Questions for Reflection:

- Do I deserve to suffer or experience joy?
- Is there something flawed in me that makes me deserve pain?
- Am I prepared to shift my beliefs and begin the journey into healing?

5. The Wisdom of Your Body

The body possesses a deep wisdom gained through millions of years of evolutionary time. It is integrative, synergistic, primitive, and wise. Accessing the wisdom of the body enables us to begin making healthy choices.

Questions for Reflection:

- If I listened to my body, what would it be telling me?

- What is my body telling me about the short-term consequences I experience as a result of my habit?
- What is my body telling me about the long-term consequences I experience or fear as a result of my habit?

6. Am I Open to Help?

There are important times in life when we need help to heal ourselves physically or emotionally. For some people, acknowledging the need for help is difficult, but essential, to begin the healing process.

Questions for Reflection:
- Can I heal my addiction on my own?
- Can I allow another person close enough to help me?
- What am I afraid will happen if I acknowledge I need help to heal my life?

7. My History of Help

People struggling with addictive behaviors become discouraged because of previous unsuccessful attempts to stop. Identifying past challenges and new incentives opens the door to healing.

Questions for Reflection:
- Have I previously sought professional help for my addiction?

- What were the factors that led to relapse or that I fear will result in my relapse now?
- Is this time different? Why?

8. Family Causes and Effects

Children are not responsible for setting their own boundaries. Our earliest experiences with setting boundaries can contribute to pain or insecurity. Becoming aware of these early experiences and how we attempt to manage the pain can help us heal.

Questions for Reflection:

- How did my early experience with addiction help me cope with my family of origin?
- What are the traits of my parents that I have rejected and internalized?
- How am I acting out my childhood stories in my current life?

9. Ecology

The environment influences the individual, and the individual influences the environment. Understanding the ecology of our lives and addiction empowers us to change.

Questions for Reflection:

- How does my environment reinforce my habit?

- Do I recognize the need to give up people and things in order to find lasting peace?
- Can I envision a life that does not include the people or environment that reinforces my addictive behaviors?

10. Issues of Trust

Addictive behaviors may create harm but are reliable. People sometimes express that a cigarette or a glass of wine is their best friend. Learning to relate more intimately with others requires healing issues around trust.

Questions for Reflection:

- What has been my experience with trust in my life?
- What are qualities other people would express that would allow me to trust them?
- What qualities am I willing to express that would enable others to trust me?

11. My Mechanisms of Defense

Recognizing a problem is the first step to solving it. We mobilize psychological defense mechanisms to avoid dealing with issues that cause us pain.

Questions for Reflection:

- What psychological defenses have I mobilized that have kept me from dealing with my addictive behavior?

- How have these defenses served me and harmed me?
- Is this the time to lower my defenses? What are the anticipated consequences?

12. The Consequences of My Addiction

We have control over our choices but not over the consequences of our choices. Putting our full attention on our current choices increases the probability that the consequences of our choices will be evolutionary.

Questions for Reflection:

- What circumstances in my present life are the unintended consequences of past choices?
- Could I foresee the consequences at the time I was making my choices?
- What are the choices I have before me now? Can I foresee the consequences they are likely to bring?

13. Patterns

Most people have an addictive behavior of choice with secondary habits that may not serve their highest purpose.

Questions for Reflection:

- In addition to my primary addictive behavior, what other habits do I recognize that are not serving me?
- What needs do these secondary habits attempt to fulfill?
- Can I envision a lifestyle that is free from both my primary and secondary life-damaging habits?

14. Cravings

Habits create emotional and physiological patterns that reinforce cravings. Learning to manage them until they fade away is important in avoiding relapses.

Questions for Reflection:

- How does it feel to have a craving?
- What has happened in the past that has led me to succumb to my cravings?
- What can I do moving forward to avoid indulging in my cravings?

15. Experiencing Anger and Rage

Boundary violations mobilize reactions. In the attempt to reestablish healthy boundaries, anger may play an adaptive role. Unfortunately, pain from the past often generates anger that is displaced upon ourselves or other innocents.

Questions for Reflection:

- What am I angry about?
- How does my anger hurt me?
- How does my anger hurt others?

16. Feeling Regret and Shame

Each of us has made choices in the past that caused pain to others or to ourselves. Releasing the regret and shame is essential to healing and transformation.

Questions for Reflection:

- What am I carrying with me from the past that is no longer serving me in the present?
- Can I acknowledge that I was doing my best from my level of consciousness at the time?
- If I knew then what I know now, how would my choices have been different?

Moving Forward

Having identified the underlying dialogue that has been directing your life choices, you now have a chance to more consciously write the next chapter. Consider that however you have arrived at this point in time and space, you have the opportunity to take a new step in a new direction. In the Brihadaranyaka Upanishad we are told,

> *You are what your deep, driving desire is.*
> *As your desire is, so is your will.*
> *As your will is, so is your deed.*
> *As your deed is, so is your destiny.*[1]

Become clear about your deepest desires and intentions to increase the likelihood that your destiny will be one of peace, harmony, and love. Take some time to savor these questions, listening to the information, knowledge, and wisdom that emerge from deeper aspects of your being.

1. What choice am I facing at this moment in my life?

We have the ability to make choices. This gift of free will differentiates people from other sentient beings. Take the time to see clearly the choices available to you right now. Notice how each choice has likely consequences. Envision the consequences of the choices you are facing, and stay tuned to the sensations of comfort and discomfort your body generates as you consider your options. These physical sensations are your body's attempt to inform you of the likely outcome of your choices.

2. If lasting happiness were the driving force behind my choices, how would I be living differently than I am?

Most of us were not encouraged to make decisions based upon what makes us happy. Most of us were taught to make choices based upon what made our caregivers, teachers, or authority figures happy. Listening to your heart, envision a life driven by the pursuit of genuine happiness.

3. If genuine and lasting love were the driving force behind my choices, how would I be living differently than I am?

Love is the memory of wholeness in which the boundaries of our individuality are less distinct. Love is the interconnectedness between all local expressions, and the underlying unity from which all things arise and return. Some say love is the opposite of fear.

Consider how your choices might be different if they were driven by the desire to reconnect with your source. Rather than desperately striving to accomplish, achieve, or acquire in order to gain another's approval, you would take those steps most likely to bring you peace and harmony. Envision a life motivated by love, knowing that you have the innate ability to generate this renewable commodity.

4. Am I ready to relinquish the belief that I am a passive victim in my life? Am I prepared to accept the responsibility that I co-create my world?

There is a story about a man who was looking for a new town to which he could relocate. He visited the wise elder of the village and asked, "What types of people live in this place?" The elder asked, "What types of people live in the place that you're from?" The man replied, "Very difficult. They were never there when you needed them. They were always looking for a handout and couldn't be trusted." The elder responded, "You'll find the same types of people in this town." Hearing this, the man continued his search.

Soon another man looking to relocate visited the village. He too sought out the wise elder and a similar conversation transpired. When asked about the people in the town he left, the man replied, "My former townspeople were delightful.

There were honest, trustworthy, and always ready to lend a hand." The wise elder affirmed that he would likely find the same types of people in this town.

With our thoughts we create our worlds. We encourage you to examine your core beliefs and see how you extract those elements of your experiences that reinforce your beliefs. Beliefs are the ideas we hold to be true. If the ones you are holding are not serving you, consider exchanging them for ones that will.

5. What is my life's purpose?

What is your contribution to the world? What are the unique talents that distinguish you? In Eastern philosophy, the concept of *dharma* implies that each human being has something unique to offer the world. When we discover our dharma, we express our gifts in service to ourselves and those affected by our choices.

If you have been struggling to find your purpose, there are clues that can help you. Ask yourself what comes naturally to you. Some people are naturally good working with children. Others are naturally athletic or good at math. If you have an innate artistic gift, consider how you can develop that into your work. Your innate talents can give you hints to your dharma.

Ask yourself what you really enjoy doing. Those things that bring you joy may hold the seeds to your role in the world. A good clue to dharma is how you experience time. If you are looking at your watch and counting the minutes until you can do something else, whatever you are doing then is unlikely to be your ultimate dharma. On the other hand, if time seems to fly by when you are engaged in a task, it may be an important clue that this is what you are meant to be doing with your life. Just as athletes sometimes talk about being in "the zone," each of us has the potential to become absorbed in what we're doing such that time loses its hold on us. Create a life that provides you the opportunity to live with passion.

Envisioning the Future

Healing and transformation require envisioning a life of balance, vitality, meaning, and purpose. Once you have done this, you can align your thoughts, words, and actions with your intentions for a better life. Envision a life in which you are making good choices, living in harmony with the people, elements, and forces around you. Picture yourself choosing to bring nourishment rather than toxicity into your body, mind, and soul. Imagine what your life would look like if you were living in service to yourself and those around you.

Make a commitment for your actions in the world to align with this vision of wholeness. We are the sum total of the choices we make in life. As creative beings, we have the capacity to make new evolutionary choices that deliver on our birthright to lead a life abundant in peace, love, and purpose.

2

Expanding the Steps to Freedom

·

"A.A. SAVED MY LIFE *nine years ago when I hit bottom,*" Sharon acknowledged. "*I now have no desire to drink or use meth, but I am questioning if I have to forever define myself as an alcoholic and drug addict. My A.A. friends tell me that kind of thinking is a very treacherous slope. Still, I wonder if it's possible to see myself now as a spiritual being who had a problem at one time, but am now capable of a deeper connection to God and to myself without alcohol or drugs playing a role.*"

⌇

*I*f you have a problem with alcohol, drugs, or another addiction, it is because at some point you had an experience with the substance or behavior that you interpreted as being more pleasurable than painful.

You may have gotten wasted for the first time as a college fresh-man, and although you threw up at the party and woke up with a headache the next day, there was something about the dive into oblivion that left you with a net positive impression. Impressions in consciousness give rise to desires, and at some point, desires spur you to action in an effort to regain the experience of pleasure.

With each indulgence the experience recruits more neural networks in the brain that reinforce the patterns. Likewise, relationships and activities that reinforce the habit become more dominant over those that do not. You choose, for example, to spend increasing amounts of time at places that reinforce your habit (bars, rave halls, and casinos), deepening the impressions that give rise to desires.

In this way, experiences generate psychological and physiological patterns that deepen the habits of behavior. To change your habits, you need to recognize the ecology you have created and create a more sustainable, balanced one.

If your life is constructed around a habit that influences everything from the friends you associate with to the music you listen to, it is not easy to break the pattern. When you're caught in a maze, you may not be able to find your way out if you wander aimlessly through the web. The best way to escape such a labyrinth is to find a new perspective outside of and above the entrapment you created.

Expansion of awareness through knowledge and experience is

the key to the door to freedom. Transforming your inner point of self-identity from a pattern of conditioned behaviors to a field of awareness—of spirit—in the world but not of the world can help you see your old problems in a new light and illuminate new and creative solutions. This process of transformation requires clarity and focus so that you can move from your conditioned past to a future of freedom.

Our experiences working with many people have convinced us that the following actions are the essential components underlying all lasting change.

1. Make a commitment to transformation.

Are you ready to change? Is this the time? Then set your eyes on the goal, and do not allow distractions to divert you.

2. Make a commitment not to repeat the mistakes of the past.

Life is for learning. Set your intention on breaking through the insanity of doing it the same way and expecting a different outcome.

3. Face the harsh reality of the present.

When you are lost, the first step is to determine, as best you can, where you are. You may be unhappy and uncomfortable with your current state, but this is your reality. Accepting it while recognizing your capacity to change is the beginning of healing.

4. See the infinite possibilities available in the present moment.

The nature of the universe is creative. As an expression of the universe, each of us has the ability to create something new. Set a different intention, make new choices, and new possibilities will emerge.

5. Envision where you want to be.

Your inner reality drives your thoughts, feelings, words, and actions. Imagine a life that provides you with the peace, love, and vitality you deserve.

6. Ask yourself what choices need to be made to actualize your vision.

Imagine that each choice orchestrates a cascade of consequences. Envision the choices that have the greatest probability of manifesting the reality you'd like to see for your life.

7. Create an action plan to execute your choices.

For your world to change, you need to translate your intentions into actions. Envision what you want to see unfold in your world and execute it. Be the change you want to see in your life.

Opening the Door

The Twelve Steps have provided a map for millions of people struggling to escape the prison of addiction. Trusting in the creative power inherent in awareness and drawing upon the seven essential components of transformation described above, let's look at the classic Twelve Steps[1] from a fresh point of view, enabling new opportunities for freedom to emerge.

STEP ONE: ——————————————————————

We admitted we were powerless over alcohol—that our lives had become unmanageable.

Most of us have good intentions but encounter resistance translating them into new behaviors. For example, you may have intended to adhere to a health-conscious diet, and for several days or even weeks, you ate the foods that were good for you and avoided those that sabotaged your goal. But then you found your resolve weakening and, after dispensing with a few guilty thoughts, indulged in the high-calorie, high-fat foods that you had been avoiding.

Or, after learning that your blood pressure was creeping higher, you made the decision to begin a regular exercise program. You joined a fitness club, bought new exercise clothes, and made it a point to spend an hour at the gym three times a week.

Then, one day, you had to work late on one of your usual exercise days, and the resolve to stay with the program dissipated.

Who has the ability to follow through on an intention and who is powerless to do so? From an Eastern perspective, each of us has two "I's." One is the "I" of the self-image or ego that is woven from the feedback we have been receiving since infancy. We develop a personality through our positions and possessions—our acquisitions and accomplishments—and project this image throughout the day in our relationships to others and to ourselves. This "I" may decide that we wish to change some behavior because it is creating some dissonance between who we are and who we want to be.

On a deeper level, our soul—the second "I"—is quietly observing our experiences and choices. Like a wave that looks into itself and discovers it is the ocean, the ego, through self-reflection and self-exploration, recognizes that its very personality emerges from a progressively nonpersonal domain of spirit.

Indeed, the conditioned "I," our ego's self-image, may be powerless over addiction, but there is another part of us over which addictive behavior has no power. The path to free yourself from addictive behavior lies in a spiritual journey of self-discovery. It requires the relinquishing of a false sense of control while embracing the awareness that the conditioned "I" is a convincing disguise. As you become increasingly intimate with your expanded self, the attachments that keep you dependent upon things outside yourself begin to loosen.

An insight expressed in *A Course in Miracles* illustrates this:

I am responsible for what I see.
I choose the feelings I experience, and I
decide upon the goal I would achieve.
And everything that seems to happen to me I ask for,
and receive as I have asked.[2]

This experience is not that of the ego but of the soul. The ego has no real power, while the soul is an expression of the field of universal intelligence that underlies everything in the objective world of form and phenomena and in the subjective world of thoughts, feelings, memories, and desires. Expanding our internal reference point from ego to soul enables us to translate our good intentions into life-supporting choices.

Hafiz, the fourteenth-century Sufi poet, expressed this shift in identity like this:

In this intricate game of love,
It is easy to become confused

And think you are the doer.
But God in His infinite certainty knows
He's the only one who should ever be put on trial.[3]

We can thus reframe the first step to say:

As a spiritual being, I recognize that my ego is not the real
me and has no real power. An ego-based life seeking security
through control, power, or approval is difficult to manage.

STEP TWO:————————————————————————

Came to believe that a power greater than ourselves could restore us to sanity.

As we recognize the two aspects to our being—ego and soul—the surrender of our constricted self to the expanded self describes the path of spiritual awakening. The power that is greater than ourselves is our own higher self. To seek this power we don't have to look for it externally. The seeker is the self, and this is a journey without distance.

The surrender of our individuality to our universality involves a transformation of our identity. We have a body comprising of the molecules we gathered from our environment. We have a mind filled with thoughts about past experiences and future anticipations. Underlying and giving rise to our minds and bodies is our soul—the ever-present witness to our experiences in the world and in our minds.

The soul is a field of potential from which the inner world and the outer world arise. From a physical perspective, scientists suggest that at a deeper level, the material world is immaterial. The physical objects that are localized in time and space are composed of atoms, which are mostly empty space. The subatomic particles that make up atoms are not things. Rather they are oscillating possibilities of energy and information.

We believe that human beings can also be seen as oscillating possibilities. Further, this field of possibilities from which form and phenomena arise has an essential uncertainty. But if there was no uncertainty nothing truly new could arise. Indeed, out of this intrinsic chaos emerge leaps in creativity.

Human consciousness has remarkably similar qualities. Although we have the tendency to express ourselves in predictable ways due to our habits of thoughts and behavior, we also have the inherent possibility to express our selves in new and unprecedented ways. Uncertainty is a fundamental principle of our lives. The only thing we have real control over is our next choice. The consequence of that choice cannot be known with certainty.

Our struggle to impose certainty on the world and its unwillingness to succumb generates anxiety. We attempt to relieve that anxiety with habits and behaviors that may be temporarily effective in reducing the fear but which have long-term negative consequences.

As we become more comfortable surrendering to the field of infinite possibilities and uncertainty, our needs to control, manipulate, seduce, and impose are lessened, and our ability to relax, create, surrender, and enjoy are enhanced. We can restate step two in this way:

Underlying and giving rise to my ego is a field of awareness with infinite possibilities. Surrendering to this field within myself, I become safe, centered, and balanced, and I am capable of making life-supporting choices.

STEP THREE: ————————————————————

Made a decision to turn our will and our lives over to the care of God as we understood Him.

The field of spirit underlying the subjective and objective world is unfathomable. Although our minds desperately seek predictability, we ultimately learn that the mystery is more powerful than any certainty we struggle to impose. In fact the spiritual path can be viewed as one of progressive surrender to uncertainty, for the known is the past, while the unknown is a field of infinite possibilities. When we desperately cling to the past, we limit our ability to create something that offers new opportunities for greater peace, love, abundance, vitality, and meaning.

We can make a decision for transformation and healing, while honoring the wisdom of the past and committing to learn from our mistakes. If we make the same choices we've made repeatedly, the future will closely resemble the past and the opportunities available in the present moment will be missed. If your current situation is painful as a result of past choices, facing the reality of the present is the most powerful and effective way to begin the healing process.

The word "God" has so often been used and at times abused in the name of conflict, prejudice, and intolerance that many people no longer associate the word with the creative power of the universe. In an effort to define the indefinable, people create an image of that which is omniscient, omnipotent, and omnipresent, often ascribing human characteristics to it. Then universal principles are codified into an organized system, most often called a religion, and believers fight about whose name or image is most accurate.

We encourage you to see beyond the "brand" to the unifying underlying spirit. In Vedic terms, we can understand the word "God" as an abbreviation for Generator, Operator, and Deliverer. Using this acronym, God is the unmanifest dimension of pure potential that gives rise to the world of creativity, maintenance, and dissolution. Acknowledging and embracing our connectedness to this expanding domain of spirit enables us to transform old life-damaging patterns into new life-affirming ones.

We can therefore reframe step three to read:

Made the commitment to expand my internal reference point, from a skin-encapsulated, ego seeking control and approval to a unique expression of universal Being.

STEP FOUR: ————————————————————

Made a searching and fearless moral inventory of ourselves.

Every human soul has light and dark sides. Each of us can be courageous and cowardly, generous and miserly, compassionate and callous. Our shadow self contains the secretive aspects of our nature that we try to keep hidden from ourselves and others. We engage in addictive behaviors to anesthetize ourselves from the conflict of these opposing qualities as they compete for expression.

Impulses that drive us to behave in ways that create pain and distress are buried in the hidden dimensions of our soul. A willingness to explore the shadow expands creativity and freedom. Acknowledging, embracing, and integrating our darkness does not make us weak. It makes us whole.

One of the most powerful tools to heal and transform the shadow is recapitulation, a method of self-review. Taking time to review our actions and noticing when we responded from fear rather than wisdom enable us to learn from our past, access creativity, and recognize the transitory nature of emotional reactions. We practice recapitulation on a daily basis and encourage you to develop the habit.

At the end of your day, right before you lay your head down on the pillow, sit up in bed and spend a few minutes quieting your mind in meditation. If you have not received formal instruction in a meditation technique, simply observe the inflow and outflow of your breath without resistance. Whenever you find your attention drifting away from your breathing, gently bring it back to your breath.

As you find yourself settling into a state of restful awareness, begin the recapitulation process by reviewing your day, beginning with the first thing you recall upon awakening. Replay the events of your day as if watching a video of your life. As you recall the day's experiences, place attention in your heart. Feel the sensations in your body as you evoke the images of your life and notice if and when you feel some discomfort. If you notice that a particular image generates distressing feelings in your heart, slow down the recapitulation process to see if you can identify what is creating your uneasiness. Use your physical signals to focus on the details of an episode with the intention on discovering what exactly about the experience generated sensations of discomfort.

If during this process you recognize that some action was left incomplete, make the commitment to take a healing step. For example, if you realize through the recapitulation process that you failed to act when it may have been beneficial or you did act in a way that caused unnecessary pain, determine what you can now do to bring peace to the situation.

Performing this process on a daily basis prevents the accumulation of unsettled issues. As you connect with your heart, if you recognize a reservoir of unresolved experiences, make the commitment today to begin clearing away any pain, regrets, recriminations, or grievances. Make a call, write a letter, set up a meeting to bring peace into your life.

If the pain, regret, or grievance is with someone who is no longer alive, come up with a creative way to bring healing into the situation. This may mean making amends with a relative or performing some charitable service. The most important principle is to do what it takes to free your heart so you are not being driven by regret, anger, humiliation, disappointment, or grievance. Then you can make choices that have the greatest likelihood of enhancing your physical, emotional, psychological, and spiritual well-being.

We may reframe step four to say:

> *I commit to exploring, healing, and transforming the hidden dimensions of my heart and soul through the regular practice of recapitulation.*

STEP FIVE: ————————————————————————

> *Admitted to God, to ourselves, and to another human being the exact nature of our wrongs.*

Each of us has a story, which we tell differently depending upon the person we divulge it to. We usually tell our story in a way that we believe will make the other person like us. When we carry self-doubt or self-loathing, we tell the story in the way that denies the truth, out of fear that the truth will invoke criticism and judgment. We then rationalize to ourselves why we hide the truth, driving the issue deeper into our shadow. If we can find someone with whom we can be completely honest and tell our story without concern for judgment or criticism, we bring light into the dark aspects that we have been denying. Through self-inquiry and sharing we can reintegrate the rejected parts of ourselves and once again feel safe and authentic.

Confession is good for the soul. Festering regrets and disappointments about others and ourselves depletes our vitality and creativity. Releasing recriminations from the dark recesses of our hearts and minds clears stagnant energy and promotes healing.

The struggle to hide unhappy secrets leads to anxiety and depression. Many addictive behaviors serve the purpose of anesthetizing the pain, conflict, and self-recrimination that accompany secrets we're harboring. Finding a safe outlet for these toxic emotions is essential.

It's a curious thing that often the issues which generate the most personal embarrassment and distress are the most universal. Self-doubt, regret, and fear of failure are nearly universal attributes, even though people often believe they are the only ones to harbor them. There is no living adult mortal who can cast the first stone.

Acknowledging our humanity while we seek to awaken our divinity relieves us of the guilty burdens that erode our soul. At one of our Chopra Center courses, we invite our guests to participate in a ritual where we ask each person to identify an issue about which they feel embarrassment or regret. We then have participants sit facing each other in two concentric circles. Each guest dons a blindfold and then whispers to another person their issue. The listener responds to the confession by saying, "I hear you and I forgive you." Then they switch roles so the confessor becomes the listener and the listener becomes the revealer. This is repeated with different partners twenty or more times until everyone has heard each other's secrets.

This is often a powerful, liberating experience for people. At first they are understandably reluctant to reveal their secrets, but they soon recognize that almost everyone is carrying something about which they feel vulnerable.

Bringing the light of awareness into the dark recesses of the shadow self frees us to move forward as conscious choice-makers rather than people being driven by regret or grievance.

We can then express a new understanding of step five as:

I commit to cultivating nourishing relationships with others and with myself, so I am able to make healthy choices without the burden of regret, resentment, or grievance.

STEP SIX:

Were entirely ready to have God remove all these defects of character.

From a Buddhist perspective, we have two primary opposing impulses. One is the impulse to separate, while the other is the impulse to unite. When we activate our discriminating mind we focus on how we differ from each other. The nature of the intellect is to identify and magnify differences through our evaluations and interpretations. To an outside observer the distinctions between Hutus and Tutsis may be insignificant, but the differences were used by some to justify the genocide of almost a million people in Rwanda. An outsider would be challenged to differentiate a Sunni from a Shiite Muslim in Iraq, but some who define themselves by their religious beliefs believe the distinctions are worth dying for.

On an individual level, each of has a repertoire of characteristics that can be labeled good or bad, right or wrong, desirable or undesirable, depending upon the context. A person who may be judged as exhibiting undesirable aggression in one setting may be considered heroic in another. There is no clear line between traits of being assertive and domineering, adaptable and inconsistent, dedicated and obsessive.

At times a trait we label as negative drives behaviors that are positive. If your insecurity about your ability to succeed compels you to create wonderful things in life, the so-called negative trait has a positive effect. If your sense of unworthiness about receiving a substantial inheritance inspires you to devote yourself to philanthropic endeavors, the dark energy empowers the light as wood feeds a fire.

We all have opposing energies. Some are divine and some are diabolical; some are sacred and some are profane. There is a place in consciousness which recognizes that having positive and negative traits does not make us flawed but makes us complete. At a deep level of your soul, you may recognize the seeds of separation and the seeds of unity. If you nurture the seeds of separation with your attention, you will go one way. If you pay attention to the dimension of your soul that integrates and embraces your opposing forces, you'll go another way.

You do not have to rid yourself of your shortcomings. In fact, it is not possible. Rather, whenever you experience the emotional turbulence generated by feelings of humiliation, insecurity, or embarrassment, you can access the real you, which transcends duality. Knowing that everyone has weaknesses and strengths, you can surrender to the sacred domain that gives rise to duality, liberating yourself from the bondage of self-importance and self-pity.

We believe the step six could benefit from a revision to keep us on a path that has the possibility of success. Here's how:

I commit to accessing the aspect of my being that embraces and transcends the duality of my nature, so I may consciously choose to express those qualities that resonate with my higher self.

It is our belief and experience that addicts are on a spiritual quest, even if they are not consciously aware of it. Their desire for ecstasy is innately spiritual. Often as a result of severe childhood pain and trauma, the addict's valuation of behaviors that provide short-term relief from the pain of life is substantially higher than most. Still, we can embrace the fundamental principles of addictive behavior and reframe the conversation in a way that is empowering.

Our perspective on the Twelve Steps is intended to unite people who see themselves as addicts and those who do not. We find that whenever our perception expands, creative opportunities for healing and transformation emerge.

STEP SEVEN: ————————————————

Humbly asked Him to remove our shortcomings.

Shift your attention to the point of awareness you hold to be "I." Notice that this "I" is the inner reference point from which your intentions and desires arise and at which all sensory experiences converge. In Vedic science this point of reference is called *ahankara*, which can be loosely translated into English as "the ego." When we experience success in manifesting our desires, our ego is reinforced and becomes more confident in its ability to exert power, maintain control, and win approval. When the ego encounters challenges in meeting its needs, it loses confidence, which is experienced in the body as anxiety or frustration.

When the ego is our internal reference point—that is, when we believe that our primary identity is the one who is desiring and experiencing—we swing back and forth between self-confidence and self-doubt.

We have an ego, and we have a soul. The ego experiences the world with its pleasures and pains declaring ownership when doing so serves its purpose and declining ownership when it does not. The soul stands in witness to our thoughts, feelings, and actions, providing the continuity to our experiences. As we deepen the understanding of our essential nature, the constricted sense of self that characterizes the ego expands to embrace and ultimately become the ever-present soul. Like a wave that thinks it stands alone until it looks within and realizes it is the ocean, the ego upholds a false sense of identity until it looks inside and realizes it is the soul.

The wave may think it is moving through its own efforts until it has a transformation in its identity and surrenders authorship to the ocean. Likewise before awakening, the ego takes credit for its accomplishments, but upon recognizing its true nature becomes lightheartedly humble.

No outer power can remove our shortcomings, any more than we can take the darkness out of light. The coexistence of opposite values is the very essence of the universe. Without positive and negative poles we would not have electricity. Without positive and negative subatomic particles, we wouldn't have matter. It is the dance between positive and negative force that propels the evolutionary flow of life.

The only way to live an authentic life is to explore, acknowledge, and embrace the dark aspects of your soul that compel you to make choices that generate pain and hardship. Acknowledging that you can be arrogant, self-centered, needy, self-righteous, and pathetic enables you to recognize when those qualities are being expressed and explore more creative ways of getting your needs met. Through self-inquiry and progressive expansion of your self-identity, your higher self becomes your internal reference. From this place of truth, knowingness, and grace, you become established in compassion, worthy of giving and receiving forgiveness.

Let's then rephrase this step seven to say:

I commit to acknowledging the light and dark elements of my nature as an expression of a deeper reality that is beyond duality. Accepting my capacity for duality and unity empowers me to make life-supporting evolutionary choices.

STEP EIGHT:

Made a list of all persons we had harmed, and became willing to make amends to them all.

Ego-based choices often occur because of our internal conversations around feelings of insufficiency. Our inner voice basically says, "I am not feeling fulfilled and require something outside myself to complete me." To satisfy my desires, I will take the steps I believe are necessary to meet my needs. In meeting my needs, I may fail to consider how my choices affect you. By focusing on what I need, I may cause you unintentional pain. At times I may recognize that my actions cause you discomfort, but relieving my discomfort takes precedence over creating yours.

The more intense the need, the more likely we are to disregard how our choices affect other people. This is certainly true when dealing with addictive behaviors. If your need to relieve anxiety with alcohol becomes more important than your need for my attention, affection, or appreciation, you will take whatever action is required, without much regard for me. If your need for money to buy your next heroin fix helps you rationalize stealing from me, my needs are relegated to a lower priority than yours.

When awareness is constricted, fulfilling our needs will most likely conflict with the needs of others. When awareness is expanded, however, we recognize that we are inextricably interwoven with each other. The arising, the fulfillment, and the consequences of actions to meet our needs are woven into an ecological network. For every need there is a most evolutionary path which offers the greatest possibility of fulfilling your needs and those around you.

If you make recapitulation a part of your practice, you will notice times when your actions disturbed the peace of those around you. If in retrospect you can envision a more creative solution than the one you resorted to at the time, use the opportunity for healing and transformation.

Consider the consequences of the choices you have made in the past, and see if you would now make different choices as a result of your experiences and understanding. Then engage in open, nondefensive conversations with people who have been hurt by your prior choices. These conversations are usually most meaningful when you already have a history of making the changes in your life that contributed to your hurtful behavior.

If you see that your addictions caused pain to your family, take steps to change your life-damaging behavior. As your choices reflect your willingness to heal and transform, approach the people who have been wounded, take responsibility for the behavior that was driven by your constricted awareness, and commit to healing the relationships through conscious life-supporting behaviors. Through the process of identifying, embracing, and healing the dark sides of our nature, we are able to heal and transform our relationships, recruiting the people in our lives to be our spiritual allies.

Our reframing of the eighth step is:

I commit to taking responsibility for the choices I have made that had unintended consequences, including creating pain for others and myself.

STEP NINE:

Made direct amends to such people wherever possible, except when to do so would injure them or others.

In Mexican Toltec teacher Don Miguel Ruiz's book *The Four Agreements,* the first agreement is to be impeccable with your word [because] the commitment to truth is important and liberating.[4] The challenge with truth is its chameleonlike nature. People consciously assign the notion of "truth" to something that they strongly believe in. We often massage the truth to rationalize behaviors born of need. Although you may acknowledge that your addiction to alcohol or drugs is not serving you or the people in your life, you may rationalize your choices—

even when they cause pain to others—because they at least temporarily alleviate your own pain.

As you awaken to the deeper understanding of who you are, you recognize that you cannot find fulfillment outside yourself. Your behaviors become less desperate, and you therefore have less need to rationalize them. It is from this platform of personal responsibility and inner peace that you are ready to heal your relationships. As your identity becomes less local and more universal, you spontaneously begin treating other people as you would wish to be treated, and you don't treat people in ways you would not want to be treated. You recognize that everyone is a mirror of your self.

The ego is perpetually asking the question, "What's in it for me?" The soul asks, "How can I help?" A fascinating paradox of life is that when we are committed to consciousness-based living, our ego takes satisfaction in being less egocentric.

There is great value in helping another. As you go through your healing, ask yourself how your new insights can help others. Consider what you are seeking in your life and look for ways to help other people meet their needs. Whatever you want, help someone else get it as well. If you are in search of love, find ways to share your love. If you are seeking success, see how you can help someone else become more successful. If you are craving forgiveness, offer your forgiveness generously.

It is also helpful to recognize that timing is key. An important skill in conscious living is paying attention to the seasons, cycles, and rhythms of life. There is a season to every purpose. A poignant scene from Nikos Kazantzakis's *Zorba the Greek* highlights the importance of timing.[5] Zorba encounters a butterfly attempting to come out from a cocoon. Because it is not moving along as fast as he would like, Zorba breathes his warm breath on it, hastening its emergence. To his horror he realizes the butterfly's wings are crumpled, and it does not have the strength to open them. It dies in his hands because of his impatience. This poignant lesson reminds us of the value of patience.

It may be that you have had an important breakthrough in your life and have made the decision to cast off old destructive behaviors and embrace new ones. It may be that you are ready to clear the past and start anew. However, the people with whom you engaged in a prior incarnation may not be ready at this time to see you in your new light. Expanding your awareness implies that you are increasingly willing to recognize that everyone is evolving at their own pace and that no one can impose their change on another.

The spiritual path is a path of self-referral. Your inner peace is not dependent upon anyone else's endorsement. From your platform of expanded awareness, you can see the interweaving of the elements of forces of nature conspiring to create the stories of life. Until you recognize that each of us is playing a role in a cosmic performance, you may not question that your character can evolve. You can read the script that you've been handed or you can improvise. You can change the plot line and bring new dimensions to your character.

Seek out the opportunities to make amends with those who have experienced pain through your less conscious interactions. Offer your apologies for choices you made that in retrospect were less than life supporting. Make a commitment that you will increasingly live in heart-centered awareness, so your choices will have maximum benefit for yourself and those affected by your choices.

If despite your best intentions and genuine commitment to heal, someone is unprepared to embrace your transformation at this time, take in the information, be present with the emotions that are generated, and use the experience as a learning opportunity. Keep your heart open even if the other person is not ready to expose theirs. Trust in the power of love and know that, in the right season, even the unforgivable can be healed.

We can express step nine in this way:

I commit to a life of healing and transformation. Through my thoughts, words, and actions, I will demonstrate my awareness of the interrelatedness of life.

STEP TEN:

Continued to take personal inventory and when we were wrong promptly admitted it.

The universe operates through polarity. Without it, there would be no movement. Still, the perpetual labeling of people, situations, circumstances, or things as good or evil, right or wrong, divine or diabolical perpetuates conflict and turmoil for individuals, communities, and nations. The inner dialogue that divides the world into right and wrong is incompatible with peace. If you engage in an ongoing dialogue of right and wrong, you will continue the soul-constricting habit of labeling yourself as good or bad, based upon your history of choices. Rather than thinking in terms of right and wrong, we encourage you to think in terms of choices made with more or less awareness. Choices made with limited awareness have a greater likelihood of extracting a toll for whatever temporary comfort or pleasure you derive. Actions made with expanded awareness are more likely to generate comfort and happiness for the person making the choice and all those affected by it.

Performing recapitulation on a daily basis will help you stay in touch with your deeper self and the archetypal energies that reside in your collective soul. Within each of us there are forces that act out of love and forces that act out of fear. In Eastern wisdom traditions these competing forces are represented as wrathful and benevolent deities. These gods do not reside outside us but within our collective soul. Like the cartoon images we watched as children, little devils and little angels sit on our shoulders competing for our attention.

Make visiting the dimension of these powerful psychological forces a part of your life. Take time on a regular basis to bring your attention within. Explore the impulses that are fed by fear, and look for ways to bring in more love. The archetypal forces seeding discontent have a divine purpose—to drive us deeper into our soul in search of peace.

The habits we engage in to anesthetize our existential pain of emptiness—alcohol, drugs, gambling, sex, food, or work—are fundamentally sacred in that they arise from an intention to reduce suffering or make life more meaningful in some way. Of course, experiencing present-moment awareness by wagering a week's salary on a horse race ultimately results in more suffering or less meaning, but still, the impulse to descend into oblivion emerges from a spiritual intention. The call to escape the prison of the individual ego is a call to transcend our isolation and experience the transcendent. The relief provided by substances or behaviors is a poor substitute for the ecstasy available through a spiritual experience. The quest is noble; the method is lacking.

As we engage in a daily practice of quieting our internal dialogue and recapitulating our choices, we may notice times when our behavior was not aligned with our higher self. These become opportunities for creativity. A situation, circumstance, or encounter may have activated an emotional response, which although immediately protective, may not have been the optimal choice for getting everyone's needs met. Reactions based upon reflexive psychological defense mechanisms serve to protect one's self-image but are usually based on fear. Therefore they often are overreactions to a perceived threat. An ego, less in need of self-protection, is capable of accessing more nuanced responses that accomplish the intended outcome without wasting precious life energy.

Fear-based responses constrict awareness. The more primitive the reaction, the less creativity we are able to access. Similarly, the more constricted our awareness is, the more likely we are to respond in fear to a threat or challenge. On the hierarchy of responses we are capable of mobilizing, the fight-or-flight reaction is most deeply rooted in our biology. A perceived threat generates the physiology that propels us to attack or run from the perceived threat. When threatened on a psychological level, we mobilize a thinly veiled fight-or-flight reaction through our defense mechanisms. We may not physically attack the offender but may seek to rake and claw our antagonist through sarcasm, criticism, name-calling, or ridicule. We may not physically run from a threat to our self-image; rather we may withdraw and withhold, becoming emotionally unavailable.

As we expand our sense of self, our need to defend or to protect becomes less. Paradoxically, as we embrace our inherent vulnerability, we become less vulnerable to the trivial slights and insults that challenge our central place in the universe. From this centered, balanced, and open inner reference point, we can make the choices most likely to generate benefit for ourselves and those touched by our decisions. When upon reflection we recognize that an earlier choice generated unnecessary pain or conflict for another, we can take steps to restore peace and harmony without an inflated sense of self-importance.

We can reframe step ten to be:

I commit to a spiritual practice of responding to life with greater awareness so my choices will be increasingly life supporting.

STEP ELEVEN:—————————————————

Sought through prayer and meditation to improve our conscious contact with God, as we understood Him, praying only for knowledge of His will for us and the power to carry that out.

Meditation is the key to healing. It is an inner journey of discovery that provides the technology to transform identity. A wave that looks within discovers its deeper, more expansive nature. The inner journey of discovery is meditation.

We are encouraged from the day of our birth to explore the outer world with its sensations, forms, and phenomena. Throughout our developmental years we are encouraged, cajoled, threatened, and bribed to master the ways of the world. Beyond mere survival, the ideals of accomplishment, achievement, and acquisition are dangled before us as the keys to happiness, freedom, and peace.

The meditative journey brings balance to life. In the ancient Upanishads of the Vedic tradition of India we're told, "As great as the infinite space is beyond, so is the space within the lotus of the heart. What is within that space should be longed for and realized." We all want abundance. We all want the ability to manifest our dreams. The pursuit of goals is intrinsic to life. To fulfill our desires we must embrace going within, connecting with our infinite creativity, and then manifesting our dreams through one-pointed intention. One-pointed intention is the skill of archers who do not allow themselves to be distracted by anything that interferes with their ability to focus on the target. Fulfillment in the world and fulfillment in ourselves are mirror images.

Meditation includes reflective self-inquiry in which we ask ourselves the deeper questions: *Who am I? What do I want? How can I use my innate talents to serve?* If I recognize I am compulsively involved in some behavior, I ask myself, *What do I hope to get out of it?* If upon reflection we recognize that the deeper need is unlikely to be met through our habitual choices, then we ask, *What other path may take me to my true goal?*

Because we believe that meditation and self-inquiry are the most essential components of a life dedicated to freedom, healing, and transformation, we will devote the entire next chapter to these practices. We can establish the importance of these principles by reframing step eleven as the following affirmation:

Through meditation and reflective self-inquiry, I commit to immersing myself in expanded awareness, thinking and behaving in the world as an expression of the universe.

STEP TWELVE: ─────────────────────────

Having had a spiritual awakening as the result of these steps, we tried to carry this message to alcoholics, and to practice these principles in all our affairs.

Ralph Waldo Emerson once said, "Who you are shouts so loudly in my ear, I can't hear what you are saying." Each of us is a magnificent multidimensional being with many facets to our nature. When the forces and elements in our lives are harmonized, the song that we sing is unique and irresistible. As we evolve in our understanding of ourselves and our relationship to the world, we have the opportunity to weave our ambiguities and contradictions into a fascinating whole. Accepting and embracing our inconsistencies and incongruities brings peace with ourselves and with others. There is nothing more attractive than natural self-acceptance.

Self-acceptance naturally infuses your being by appealing to your higher, more expansive impulses, while still acknowledging your more constricted ones. Through inquiry you can access the underlying threads that weave your life. Find a quiet place and spend a few minutes listening to the answers that emerge from your heart in response to the questions that follow, which we call the "Soul Profile."

1. What is my life purpose?

Ask yourself what is driving your thoughts and actions at the deepest level of your being.

2. What would I like to contribute to the world?

What would you like to leave behind that reflects the best of who you are?

3. Who are my heroes?

What people or qualities of people would you like to emulate? They may be people in your present life or historical characters who have motivated you to reach higher and express the best aspects of your nature.

4. What words could I use to describe a peak experience?

A peak experience is an event when you momentarily transcended time and space. It may occur while witnessing extraordinary beauty in nature, while hearing a rapturous piece of music, or while making love. What words come to mind that describe an experience that was beyond words?

5. What are the three most important qualities I look for in a friend?

Consider the characteristics of a person in whose presence you feel so safe that you would be willing to reveal yourself fully.

6. What are my unique talents?

Each of us has innate abilities that express the essence of who we are. What are you naturally good at? What comes easy to you?

7. What are the best qualities I express in my personal relationships?

When we feel centered and safe within ourselves, we are capable of projecting ourselves in ways that enrich and support the healing and personal development of our friends, acquaintances, and family members.

Look within yourself and see the grace, power, and freedom that are your birthright. Realizing that you have divinity within you, commit to aligning your choices with the qualities of your soul. Carry this map of your sacred self with you, and refer to it regularly so your life path will be in accordance with your deepest evolutionary intentions. Thus, we can restate the final step as:

I commit to exploring the sacred dimensions of my soul and expressing my higher qualities in my relationships with others and myself.

Seeking ecstasy is a sacred quest. For those wasting away in the prison of separation, any means to escape, even temporarily, is comprehensible. Those imprisoned in an addiction use their substance of choice for a temporary furlough. In the next chapters we offer you freedom.

The Freedom from Addiction Program

WE BELIEVE IN THE POWER of awareness and the importance of perceiving the world through new eyes. Still, it is in the day-to-day living of life that healing and transformation occur. When you practice conscious living, you enable new patterns to emerge that increase the possibility of freedom, joy, love, and ecstasy. In this section we share the approaches we offer our guests at the Chopra Center. These are designed to quiet inner turbulence, encourage the elimination of toxicity from your life, awaken vitality, and heal your heart. Through these steps, you can reestablish a deep and nurturing connection between your body, heart, mind, and soul.

3

The Power of Silence

AS A LEADING BUSINESSMAN in his community, Sam was adept at entertaining. He seemed to have an innate capacity to drink more than his peers without losing total control, and he liked the lowering of boundaries he felt with alcohol. What he didn't like was his irritable mood when he wasn't drinking and his cravings that began midafternoon.

Although acknowledging he had a problem, Sam was unwilling to accept his family doctor's label of alcoholism or the need for inpatient treatment. When he visited the Chopra Center, he was honest about his reluctance to give up drinking completely but open to trying something to pull him back from what he called "the edge."

Since he was not prepared to make a major shift in his

life, we made the one recommendation we believe offers the greatest potential benefit. We taught him to quiet his mind in meditation and asked him to practice it twice daily for the next forty days.

*I*n our decades of experience working with people attempting to free themselves from addictions, we have found meditation to be the most powerful tool to change negative patterns. In fact we have never witnessed a person relapse when they are meditating regularly. According to Buddhism, we create the world with our thoughts. If our minds are filled with turbulent thoughts, our life experiences will tend to be turbulent. If our minds are quiet and focused, our experience of ourselves and the world around us mirrors this inner state of centered awareness.

Addictive behaviors are attempts to neutralize uncomfortable thoughts and the feelings associated with them. Meditation is the most important natural technology we know of to soothe the mind and access the power of silence contained within it. We all have a natural aptitude to experience inner peace, but most of us need some help to awaken this ability. As a vehicle to expand consciousness, meditation is the best habit you can cultivate. It can ultimately fulfill and replace all other addictions.

The Katha Upanishads tell us, "When the five senses are stilled, when the mind is stilled, when the intellect is stilled, that is called the highest state by the wise." Through the inward journey of meditation, we discover this state of being that gives rise to and transcends our individuality. Bringing silence into life enriches our body and mind and provides direct access to our soul—the silent, ever-present source of our desires, talents, and creativity.

Meditation helps you become self-centered in the best possible way, while expanding your sense of self at the same time. Experiencing yourself in more expanded ways catalyzes healing. Through the power of silence you can discover new solutions to old problems and free yourself from life-constricting patterns.

The Biology of Stress

The boundaries of your body are rich with nerve endings designed to inform you when something invades your personal borders. The pain you feel when you step on a tack, bump your head on a low cabinet, or burn your fingers on a match provides strong signals to withdraw from the offending agent that has crossed the threshold of your individuality without your permission.

The evolutionary basis of this reaction is obvious. If we do not protect our personal boundaries, we cannot maintain our individuality. From amoebas to elephants, living entities have an innate disposition to defend themselves through retreat or attack.

Human beings have benefited from millions of years of biological evolution and have developed sophisticated physical defense mechanisms that mobilize us when we feel threatened. Known as the "fight-or-flight response," this survival reaction compels us to take aggressive action when we perceive danger. American physiologist Walter Cannon first described it in the 1930s, and we now understand both the short-term benefits and longer-term risks of this primitive response.

Governed by the nervous and endocrine systems, the fight-or-flight response redirects all available life energy to protect the individual. When you feel threatened, your pupils automatically dilate to let in more light. Your heart beats faster and harder to deliver more oxygen and energy to your body's tissues. Blood flow is spontaneously diverted from your digestive tract to the muscles of your arms and legs, because digesting your lunch is not a high priority if you are at risk of becoming another creature's next meal. Your sweat glands release perspiration to keep you from overheating, while your glucose levels rise because of complex shifts in blood-sugar-regulating hormones. The stress hormones adrenaline and noradrenaline are released from your adrenal glands, and they enable you to mobilize and use energy.

Activating the fight-or-flight response when a tiger is about to pounce is clearly adaptive and potentially life saving. Given the limited natural defenses of a human being—we don't have ferocious fangs or sharp claws—quickly getting into gear to run or fight allowed us in bygone eras to live another day while we developed the technology to exert dominion over our environment.

In modern times, other than on the battlefield, the experience of being physically threatened is a relatively rare event. It's not very often that we have to run for our lives or chase prey to survive. Still we have the tendency to express aspects of the fight-or-flight response whenever our needs are not being met. The urge to lash out or escape is just below the surface when we're stuck in rush-hour traffic, open a phone bill that seems too high, or discover a scratch on our new car. These annoyances in life have a cumulative effect on our physiology, pushing us incrementally toward activation of the response, but never actually releasing the pressure that builds up within.

If we look at the major health challenges of modern life, many may be the outcomes of the inappropriate activation of fight-or-flight reactions. Raising your blood pressure, accelerating your heart rate, and increasing the output of your cardiovascular system may be helpful responses if a tiger is chasing you in the jungle, but they put you at risk of an early heart attack if you are an overworked attorney. Shunting blood away from your digestive track into your arms and legs is useful if you're scampering up a tree to escape a pack of wolves, but it predisposes you to digestive distress if you are pulled over for speeding while trying to get to your daughter's recital on time. Rising blood-sugar levels that deliver energy to your tissues are helpful when you are hunting down a wildebeest, but they contribute to diabetes and obesity when you consume high-caloric foods and drinks to keep your energy sustained during an all-night work effort. The stress hormones, adrenaline and noradrenaline, excite your mind and intensify your metabolism, which is useful if you must react suddenly to a grizzly bear that wants to reclaim its cave. However, if your adrenal glands are pumping out these hormones because you are over your head financially and in jeopardy of going bankrupt, you will experience unhealthy anxiety and insomnia. Addiction to alcohol or drugs—both prescription and nonprescription—as well as other compulsive habits often develop as an effort to mollify these uncomfortable symptoms of stress.

For those times that we actually need to battle or escape in order to survive, we value the fight-or-flight response as part of our physiological repertoire, but we cannot afford the physical or emotional price of being perpetually prepared to react aggressively to perceived threats. The wear and tear on mind and body of perceiving the world as threatening makes us sick, may lead to maladaptive behavior, and can eventually kill us. Fortunately just as we have the intrinsic propensity to activate this response, we also have the natural ability to deactivate it.

The Physiology of Restful Awareness

Scientists who study the brain divide neurological function into two major categories: voluntary and involuntary. Buttoning your shirt, talking on the phone, and running to an airport gate make use of your voluntary nervous system. Regulating blood pressure, maintaining body temperature, and moving food through the digestive system are governed by the involuntary nervous system.

Until the latter half of the twentieth century, brain scientists believed we could consciously influence the voluntary, but not the involuntary, side of our nervous systems. Beginning in the 1950s, however, physiologists began reporting on people who seemed to possess unique abilities. Zen Buddhist monks were observed to raise their core body temperatures through a mental practice. Mind-body masters in India were able to slow their heart rates by way of self-regulating yogic techniques. Others could dramatically reduce their breathing rates and depths through meditation. At first these reports were dismissed as anomalies with little relevance to our understanding of human biology. As Western culture opened its mind to things Eastern, however, scientists became curious about the physiology of meditation and yoga. During the 1960s and 1970s college students around the world learned a variety of consciousness-expanding meditation techniques and began reporting beneficial changes in their minds and bodies.

These claims attracted the interest of physiologists and medical doctors. Researchers at Harvard, MIT, and Stanford hooked new meditators up to EEG equipment, heart-rate devices, skin galvanometers, and respiratory monitors. They analyzed the participants' blood for shifts in hormone levels, and assessed their psychological functioning with batteries of tests. It was discovered through these investigations that people have the ability to alter their physiology in ways that had not been believed possible. These changes were unique enough that some researchers began calling the meditation experience a fourth state of consciousness beyond waking, dreaming, and sleeping. The scientific term suggested was a wakeful hypometabolic state. We like the simpler expression of restful awareness.

Through simple shifts in attention and intention, meditators are able to slow their heart rates, reduce their breathing patterns, and lower their blood pressure. They can reduce their levels of stress hormones and create coherent brain waves. We now know that almost anyone can learn to voluntarily influence his or her involuntary nervous system. This response benefits the body, mind, and soul of a person. It is particularly helpful for people seeking to escape the prison of addiction.

The Physical Benefits of Restful Awareness

Meditation provides benefits on multiple levels—physical, psychological, and spiritual. This multidimensional value to human life has been described for thousands of years in Eastern wisdom traditions. Scientific studies over the past forty years have affirmed that taking time to quiet the mind and relax the body generates health-promoting changes.

In terms of physical health, the regular practice of meditation affects every system in the body. Meditation can soothe irritable bowel disease, reduce the frequency of migraine headaches, and enhance immune function.[1-3] Over time it can reduce the risk of hypertension and improve cardiac function in people with coronary heart disease.[4,5] A meditation practice can reduce the need for analgesic medication in people with chronic musculoskeletal pain conditions and in those suffering with cancer.[6,7]

Quieting Emotional Turbulence with Restful Awareness

On the level of emotions, studies have shown that meditation can help reduce both anxiety and depression.[8,9] With a decrease in worry and sadness, people are less inclined to use drugs, alcohol, or mood-regulating medications to modulate their emotions. Meditation helps reduce the level of emotional commotion by quieting the inner dialogue that generates turbulence.

Our inner world of thoughts, feelings, memories, and desires determines the quality of our lives. For most of us, our sense of self is dependent upon how comfortable or uncomfortable we feel in our profession and in our relationships. The "father of psychoanalysis," Sigmund Freud said, "Love and work are the cornerstones of our humanness." At every moment we engage in a running dialogue with ourselves about our jobs and relations. Meditation serves to interrupt this thought traffic temporarily and to enable the emergence of new creative view-points that may not have previously been considered.

Understanding the nature of mental activity makes it easier to appreciate the value of quieting the mind in meditation. If you observe your mind, you will notice that every thought that arises is either in consideration of something that has occurred in the past or in anticipation of something that might happen in the future. In the traditional meditation writings of India, the mind is kept active by continuously cycling through three stages. In one stage the mind registers an impression. Because of this impression, the mind then moves into the second stage in which it generates an intention to engage either more or less in the experience that generated the impression. The intention leads to the third stage, which is to perform some action or behavior. This action is known in Sanskrit as *karma*, a word that is famil-iar to most Westerners. As a result of the action, new impres-sions are registered, resulting in new intentions and new actions.

This cycle of **action → impression → intention → action** is known in Vedic and Buddhist traditions as the "cycle of karma." It is what keeps us behaving in predictable ways with regard to situations, circumstances, people, and things. It is at the root of all habits, both life supporting and life damaging. To free our-selves from habitual behaviors, we have to free ourselves from the cycle of karma. This cannot occur solely through conscious intention, because the impressions are deeper than our con-scious mind.

The fuel that keeps the mental cycle going is meaning. The meaning we assign to an experience triggers memories and feelings, which lead to associations and intentions. For example, you are walking in the park and you see a golden retriever puppy. The dog reminds you of a puppy you had as a child. The memory and feelings surrounding the puppy activate other thoughts about your childhood. This reminds you of the time your raging father kicked your dog because it soiled the carpet. The feelings provoked by this memory are uncomfortable, so you decide it would be a good idea to stop at the bar on the way home to have a drink. From impressions arise desires, which provoke new actions.

Meditation interrupts the mental cycle by introducing an impression that does not carry any compelling meaning. That impression can be following your breath, watching a candle, doing some free-form movement, or repeating a mantra. Regardless of the actual method you use, the value of effective meditation is to momentarily quiet the incessant activity of your mind. When your mind slips into the gap between thoughts, the body also quiets down. The experience is one of mental peace and physical relaxation. This is restful awareness.

The subjective experience of restful awareness is one of relaxed wakefulness. When the mind is active, we are focused on something internally or externally generated. We might be conscious of a thought or a feeling, a memory or a desire. We might be conscious of a sound, sensation, sight, taste, or smell. These inner or outer experiences engage our attention and generate emotional reactions to whatever is occupying our mind.

During meditation the mind is wakeful but disengaged from internal or external objects of attention. The experience of restful awareness brings peace to the mind and tranquility to the body. Of greater importance, the centering achieved in meditation extends into periods of activity. Most regular meditators notice greater emotional stability throughout the day.

Repetitive thoughts that restrict our perspective and limit our creativity compel us to seek temporary relief through addictive behaviors. Meditation offers a technology to access new perspectives. A balanced mind, unencumbered by anxiety and turbulence, is more powerful and creative. Disengaging the mind provides admission to the freedom and creativity that resides in the gap between our conditioned thought patterns. Alternating activity with regular immersion into silence cultivates healing, creativity, and balance. The peace we gain in meditation manifests in our thoughts, words, and actions.

Meditation to Awaken the Soul

The regular experience of restful awareness through meditation provides physical benefits to the body through its natural ability to neutralize the physiological imbalances caused by stress. Meditation also helps improve one's psychological state by reducing the mental turmoil associated with worry, nervousness, and insomnia. These advantages alone support the value of meditation as a tool for healing and transformation. Still, meditation's traditional role is as a technology for spiritual development, and it is here we find its most profound value to free us from negative habits.

A spiritual path is one that leads us from suffering to peace. Life is brief and interspersed with challenges. Every human being goes through times of confusion during which we experience anxiety and insecurity about the next step to take. A spiritual practice provides an underlying peace that enables us to feel connected to a dimension of our being that transcends the confusion-generating distress. Whether we call this domain of life God, spirit, nature, creative intelligence, or consciousness is of minor consequence, despite the religiously motivated battles that have been fought for millennia over its name. What is important is having access to this realm of awareness through direct experience.

In the process of becoming individuals we become attached to ideas, people, and things presented to us by the world. Our self-identity—our ego—develops through our relationships to objects outside us. In early childhood we generate our sense of "I-ness" through our connection to family members. This sense of "I" soon expands through our relationships to places and things—our toys, our pets, our schools. As we mature we embrace ideas about the world and ourselves. Through feedback from people around us, we may conclude we are smart or dumb, pretty or ugly, fast or slow, nice or nasty. We may assume ownership over religious and political ideas, identifying ourselves as Christian or Muslim, liberal or conservative. As we become adults, our identity is further defined through our roles and responsibilities: "I'm a lawyer," "I'm a schoolteacher," "I'm a mother."

We play a multiplicity of roles and assume ownership over an uncountable number of things and ideas that change over the course of our lives. The core spiritual question is, *Who am I in the midst of my positions, possessions, and beliefs?* This question is essential because we can have no lasting peace as long as our identity is rooted in the field of change. If my identity is defined by my position in an organization, who am I when I am no longer in that position? If my sense of self depends upon my relationship to another person, who am I when the relationship ends?

The spiritual value of meditation is in the expansion of our internal reference point from identification with roles, things, and beliefs to the aspect of our being that is simply aware. My ever-present witnessing awareness provides the continuity for my experiences in the world, but transcends any and all objects of identification. When Siddhartha Gautama became the Buddha, he was asked by his disciples to define himself. Was he a god? Was he a prophet? Was he a saint? The enlightened master humbly declared that the most honest way to answer the question was simply to say, "I am awake."

The shift in internal reference occurs spontaneously through the regular practice of meditation, during which we have increasingly clear experiences of awareness without mental activity. The direct experience of "I am awake," begins to infuse our nonmeditating activities. We become more aware of our underlying consciousness even as we play our roles in the world. Regular experience of restful awareness cultivates the psychology of a quiet, wakeful mind and a comfortable body. It enables a state of internally self-generated peace that is independent of external sources. From this platform of restful awareness, we lose the compulsion to alter our consciousness through drugs or alcohol, because such substances negatively impact the state of inner peace.

Getting Started with Meditation

There are many roads to silence. Without any formal technique, most people have had glimpses of the gap between thoughts through "breath-taking" experiences. A magnificent sunset, a beautiful rainbow, or an astonishing mountain vista has the capacity to bring you fully into the present and momentarily quiet your mental chatter. Listening to a Bach canon, receiving a wonderful massage, enjoying a delicious meal, or having orgasmic sex may also temporarily still your mind and relax your body.

A meditation practice provides a reliable pathway into restful awareness, independent of your circumstances. Having direct access to the silence beyond the chaos of the outer or inner worlds offers a reliable ally in our quest for peace.

At the Chopra Center, we teach our guests a practice known as "Primordial Sound Meditation." This is an ancient technique that utilizes a specially chosen mantra based upon one's birth time, place, and date. Using this technique, we find that anyone, regardless of previous experience, religious background, or age, can quickly learn to quiet their inner banter and relax. We have over seven hundred teachers certified as Primordial Sound Meditation instructors around the world, so most people have access to this practice (see the Resource section to find a teacher near you).[10]

For those readers who cannot easily find one of our trained instructors, we suggest a beginning meditation using your breath and a simple yet effective mantra. We call this the "So-Hum" technique.

So-Hum Meditation Technique

1. Find a comfortable place to sit where you will not be disturbed.
2. Close your eyes and take a few slow, deep breaths.
3. Survey your body and adjust your position so you are not feeling any tension in your muscles.
4. Begin observing the inflow and outflow of your breath.

5. Introduce the internal thought "So" on each inhalation and the thought "Hum" on each exhalation.

6. Once you have established some rhythm to the silent repetition of So-Hum, release your attention on the breath.

7. When you realize you have stopped thinking the mantra and have been lost in trains of thought, gently shift your attention back to the mantra.

8. When you realize your awareness has gone outward to a sound in your environment, gently bring it back to the mantra.

9. Treat the interruption of thoughts or noises with an inner attitude of "Whatever happens during my meditation is okay."

10. Practice the meditation for about fifteen to twenty minutes twice each day, in the morning and the evening.

Some General Meditation Tips

Be Aware of the Mantra

Repetition of the So-Hum mantra is effortless. Silent repetition of the mantra does not require that you pronounce it clearly in your mind; rather, you just need to have a vague sense of the sound as a vibration or impulse. As the mantra appears to change its rate, rhythm, or pronunciation, allow it to happen without exerting control over the process.

1. Allow Your Thoughts to Come and Go

New meditators often express the concern that they are having too many thoughts. Thoughts are a natural component of meditation, and it is not possible to forcibly stop thinking. There will be many times in every meditation during which your mind drifts away from the mantra to other thoughts. You may find yourself thinking about something that has happened in the past or something you are anticipating happening in the future. You may find yourself thinking about sensations in your body or sounds in your environment.

Whenever you become aware that your attention has drifted away from the So-Hum mantra, gently shift it back. Whether you are thinking about where you're going for dinner, about a movie you saw last night, about issues at work, or about some profound personal realization, effortlessly return your attention to the mantra when you realize you have drifted off into thoughts.

2. Don't Fight Sleep if It Comes

If your body is tired when you sit to meditate, you may fall asleep. Don't fight it. Meditation is an opportunity for your body and mind to rebalance, so if you need to sleep, do so. When you awaken, sit up and meditate using the So-Hum mantra for about ten minutes.

If you find yourself falling asleep in most of your meditations, you are probably not getting enough rest at night. Start exercising regularly during the day, minimize your caffeine consumption, do not use alcohol to sedate you, and try to be in bed with the lights off by 10 p.m. We'll talk more about an ideal daily routine in the next chapter.

3. Surrender into the Gap

As your mind quiets during meditation, you will experience moments when there is the absence of thoughts with the retention of awareness—no mantra, no thoughts, yet wakefulness. With regular practice, the clear awareness you glimpse during meditation begins to permeate your life outside of meditation. The relaxation you gain while meditating extends into your activity.

Empowering Your Intentions with Silence

Over the past fifteen years we have cared for tens of thousands of people seeking to make healthier choices. The challenge of translating our good intentions into choices is universal. We have witnessed, and therefore believe, that the most powerful means to empower our intentions is through the regular practice of meditation. Like an archer poised with an arrow pulling back on a bow, taking time to quiet the mind enables us to become focused on our targets and to provide the energy to manifest our desires.

Most people who come to the Chopra Center to transform unhealthy habits into healthy ones are successful, at least for a time. When we see people who were initially able to change their behaviors but have subsequently relapsed, we always begin with one question: Are you still meditating twice a day? Again, we have never seen a person relapse who is meditating regularly. Meditation provides the foundation for a conscious commitment to healing and transformation. We encourage you to take the time to quiet your mind on a daily basis for at least fifteen minutes, ideally for thirty minutes twice a day.

4

Detoxifying Your Body, Mind, and Soul

MURIEL KNEW IT WAS TIME to stop smoking. After a pack a day for ten years, she had become accustomed to rationalizing her habit. But with her incessant dry cough and increasingly difficult scramble to find a place to smoke, she was ready to quit.

She enrolled for a week at the Chopra Center, where she was encouraged to give up her morning caffeine and evening wine, while she received daily herbalized oil massages and healthy vegetarian meals. Along with her twice-daily meditations and yoga sessions she drank purifying herbal teas and chewed on cinnamon sticks whenever she had a strong urge to light up. Her nicotine fits felt like hell by the third day, but she resolved to keep going. By the end of the week, she could go hours without even thinking about smoking, and six months later, she no longer had the urge to smoke.

Novelist Tom Robbins once said there are only two mantras in life—yum and yuck. There is a deep truth to this humorous insight, for everything we experience ultimately either increases our level of comfort or diminishes it. From this perspective, our goal is to ingest more yum and less yuck.

We can have four possible outcomes from any choice in life. In one scenario the initial experience is pleasurable, but the longer-term consequences are painful. Shooting up heroin, snorting a line of cocaine, eating an entire chocolate cheesecake on your own, or having a passionate one-night stand with your best friend's partner are examples of initial pleasure leading to eventual pain.

In the second group of possible outcomes are experiences that defer immediate pleasure with the expectation of longer-term benefit. Studying for a final exam, preparing for a marathon, creating a household budget, and making regular contributions to a retirement plan fall into this category.

In the third group are choices that have both short- and longer-term negative consequences. There are not a lot of obvious incentives for this scenario, but one who is feeling deeply depressed, remorseful, or self-critical may engage in destructive behaviors that generate both immediate and chronic pain. Driving recklessly, intentionally putting one's hand through a window, and making a suicidal gesture are examples of this distorted thinking. Even in these situations, the action is usually motivated by the hope that the behavior will in some way reduce suffering. Sadly the long-term health consequences of a failed self-destructive act may make life more painful rather than less.

The fourth and most desirable category includes choices that provide benefits immediately and over time. These are the most life-supporting choices we can make, for they generate, rather than deplete, physical and emotional vitality. A daily meditation practice, a balanced exercise program, a delicious nourishing diet, and loving relationships fall into this class.

Learning to make choices that bring lasting pleasure is the secret to a life of peace and well-being. Our personal lessons usually have the greatest impact on our future choices, but it has been said that a foolish person learns from his own mistakes, whereas a wise one learns from the mistakes of others. Let's explore what others have learned about maximizing nourishment and minimizing toxicity.

The Importance of Detoxifying

Detoxification is an essential component of the Chopra Center method. Whether a person is carrying physical or emotional toxicity, it is one of our core premises that releasing whatever is inhibiting the free flow of vital energy in the body and mind contributes to health and happiness. We have identified four fundamental components to a successful detoxifying process: identification, mobilization, elimination, and rejuvenation.

In the 5,000-year-old healing tradition of India known as Ayurveda, an elegant program for detoxification is described. Despite the ancient origins of this purification system, the basic principles of this approach are undeniably relevant to our current worldview.

The most important concept in Ayurveda is *agni*, which translates directly into English as "fire." The words "ignite" and "ignition" derive from the Sanskrit word *agni*. Agni is the inner fire that digests your experiences and transforms them into the substance of your mind and body. When your agni is strong and robust, you can metabolize toxicity into nourishment; if your agni is weak, however, you will convert nectar into poison.

Health and Disease

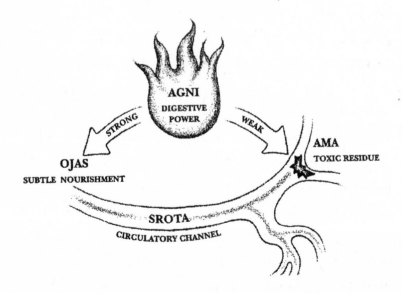

Over time a weak agni leads to the accumulation of undigested residues of experience, known in Ayurveda as *ama*. These toxic residues build up and begin to interfere with the circulation of vital energy in the body. Accumulated ama leads to fatigue, depression, chronic pain, indigestion, and immune imbalance, and provides a breeding ground for illness.

We can think of ama on multiple levels. Physically, ama can be seen as the accumulation of incompletely metabolized food. If you ingest more fat or calories than your body needs, you will deposit cellulite in your tissues or cholesterol in your blood vessels. Illness may eventually manifest because of the accumulated fat in your arteries.

If you have not fully processed an emotional experience, you may carry the residue of the painful emotion as persistent grief, hostility, or regret. The undigested feelings keep you responding in predictable patterns that inhibit you from being fully present in your current relationships. This is an expression of emotional ama.

It is also possible to carry the residue of a toxic belief. If you were raised with ideas about yourself or the world that limit your ability to generate success, happiness, and love, these beliefs can be viewed as psychological ama. Releasing toxic ideas allows nourishing information to occupy your mind.

There can be life-damaging consequences of material ama on people's lives. A person may extend himself to buy a larger house and assume a bigger mortgage. He then struggles each month to make the payments, restricting any sense of financial freedom or abundance. The stress created can be seen as financial ama in which more possessions were ingested than could be digested. Over time it will generate emotional or physical distress.

Agni is a valuable metaphor for essential life principles. For example, if you want a healthy fire burning in your campground to cook your food and keep you warm, you will need the right balance of fuel and air. Too much air, and the fire can blow out. Not enough air, and the fire will be oxygen starved. If the amount of fuel exceeds the capacity for the fire to metabolize it, smoke is generated, and in the end you are left with charred remains. According to Ayurveda, air represents change, and fuel represents stability. Evolution progresses along the steps of change and stability. Too much change or too much stagnation inhibits healthy evolution. A healthy life is dependent upon the dynamic balance between new experiences and consistency. When we are able to maintain this balance, we feel enthusiastic about life and naturally avoid unhealthy habits. When we experience too much change, we may use substances to reduce anxiety. When we are not having enough new experiences, we may use substances to overcome our monotony and boredom.

A brightly burning fire generates heat and light. In human terms, when the heat we generate is appropriate, we radiate warmth, love, and compassion to those around us. If we are burning too hot we become irritable and critical, emotionally scorching the people around us. If our inner fire is weak, we are perceived as cold and aloof. The light from our inner agni dispels the darkness around us. The insights that derive from a healthy agni illuminate our path so we are less likely to stumble over obstacles that confront us.

Agni teaches us that the inability to metabolize an experience in the past creates a lingering negative influence in the present. This is the essence of ama. Stopping the inflow of new toxicity and identifying, mobilizing, and eliminating existing ama are the essential steps of purification.

Reducing Toxic Intake

Classical yoga philosophy encompasses the practice known as *Pratyahara*. *Pratya* means "drawing back" or "retreating," while *ahara* means "nourishment." *Pratyahara* means "withdrawing from the usual sensory nourishment that feeds the mind." This is the launching point for detoxification.

Engaging in a sensory experience generates psychological, emotional, and physical shifts. If the net effect of an experience is interpreted as pleasurable, it naturally lays down a memory that generates a desire for more. The process is the same whether the sensory experience is a hot fudge sundae, a relaxing meditation, or a line of cocaine. The physiological changes predispose to dependency on the external source of pleasure. When the source of the enjoyment becomes unavailable, feelings of discomfort or discontent are generated, motivating actions to fill the void.

Using the Power of Your Intention

The technique of Pratyahara introduces a new element into the process—the power of intention. When we want something that we perceive is being withheld, we experience a lowering of our self-esteem in addition to the deprivation. The inner chemistry of feeling out of control contributes to the distress and enhances the craving for the object we think will provide relief. If we can shift our mind-set from something "being taken away" to something we are "giving up," the act of relinquishment generates positive neurochemistry.

This is the essence of Pratyahara—shifting into the intention of letting go and seeing it as an act of empowerment. Sensory fasting for a period of time resets the physiology, allowing for internally generated chemicals of comfort. It allows our mental and physical agnis to digest obstructions left over from the past, enabling life-supporting energy to flow.

Practicing Pratyahara

Serious addictions, like alcoholism and narcotic dependency, usually require a more controlled setting in which the temptations to indulge in life-damaging habits are reduced. For the less-consumptive habits you want to release, Pratyahara provides a framework to let go. Let's see how this plays out if you are trying to break your daily habit of smoking marijuana.

A Weekend Without

Make a date with yourself to implement your intention. Like any important event, it will take some preparation to make certain that things unfold the way you plan. Define the time and space you will devote to the release of your habit. It is usually difficult to maintain the focus required if you are involved in your customary activities. Therefore it is best to set aside a weekend when you are not working or beginning a vacation. For example, make the commitment that beginning Saturday morning at sunrise, you will give up your cannabis for the next forty days.

Having chosen a date, clear out any obvious seductions that may present themselves while you are shifting your mind-set. Remove any and all stashes from your personal space. If you have friends with whom you routinely use cannabis, do not make plans to be with them until you sense a new pattern has formed in your mind and body.

Set up a schedule of activities that you will follow when you start the detoxification process so you do not have time to be bored or frustrated. Choose behaviors that are purifying and nourishing. Possibilities include:

- Going for a hike
- Taking a long bike ride
- Working out at a fitness center
- Visiting a museum or an art gallery

• Taking a yoga class
• Getting a massage
• Cooking a meal for you and your non-drug-using friends
• Taking an art, music, or acting class

As you create your releasing schedule, make the appropriate appointments or reservations and acquire the necessary supplies or equipment you'll need. Make a trip to the local natural foods store to stock up on healthy snacks. Buy yourself a yoga outfit to wear to your first class. Purchase the ingredients for the delicious healthy meals you'll be preparing.

Focus your intention for the entire weekend on one thing only: detoxification. Avoid all recreational chemicals. Consider the information that you are ingesting through all your senses, and favor nourishing input that relaxes or encourages you. Arrange to spend time with people you like but are not part of your usual circle of friends. This might be a good time to meet your sister for dinner or reconnect with an old friend you haven't seen in a while. Experience something new that is interesting and inspiring. Establishing new patterns is the most effective way to overcome old ones.

Detoxing Your Body

Simplifying your diet during a weekend of detoxification allows you to redirect your energies to the metabolism of undigested experiences from the past. Even if you can only manage this for a couple of days, a simplified diet will help empower your detoxifying intention. If you can continue it for a week, you are certain to succeed.

According to yogic philosophy, certain foods are easier to digest than others and are preferred while undergoing a purification program. In general, foods that are derived from the vegetable kingdom, are freshly harvested, and are low in calories are more detoxifying than those that come from animals, are packaged, and are rich in calories. For the initial days of your purification program, try simplifying your diet by eating more fresh fruits in season and lightly steamed or sautéed vegetables. Avoid animal products and processed and highly refined foods.

Easy-to-Digest Foods That Support Detoxification

- Red lentil, split yellow pea and mung dhal soups (available at Indian and Middle Eastern food markets)
- Steamed broccoli, carrots, zucchini, asparagus, Brussels sprouts, cabbage, beets
- Steamed greens—spinach, chard, beet greens
- Basmati rice, quinoa, millet and barley
- Light vegetable soups
- Spices: ginger, cumin, coriander, fennel
- Flaxseeds, sesame seeds, sunflower seeds, and pumpkin seeds
- Poached apples and pears; cooked apricots, prunes, and figs
- Fresh berries—raspberries, blueberries, blackberries

Foods Best Reduced or Eliminated During Detoxification

- Aged cheeses
- Milk, cream; *clarified butter (ghee) in small amounts is okay*
- Animal products
- Refined sugar
- Refined white flour products
- Alcohol
- Caffeine
- Chocolate
- Ice cream

Herbal teas and freshly squeezed juices help cleanse the system. Freshly made ginger tea, prepared by grating a teaspoon of gingerroot per pint of hot water, is purifying at all levels of the digestive tract. Peppermint or spearmint, cinnamon, or chamomile can be refreshing and detoxifying. The Chopra Center has formulated a number of balancing and detoxifying herbal teas based upon core Ayurvedic principles (see Professional Resources).

Guests participating in our weeklong detoxification program at the Chopra Center are encouraged to comply with the following general guidelines:

- Favor freshly prepared, nutritious, and appetizing foods; reduce canned foods and leftovers.
- Favor lighter foods such as rice, soups, and lentils.
- Favor freshly steamed or lightly sautéed vegetables.
- Avoid fried foods.
- Avoid ice-cold foods and drinks.

- Reduce your intake of dairy products.
- Avoid fermented foods and drinks. This includes vinegar, pickled condiments, cheeses, and alcohol.
- Keep oils to a minimum other than the prescribed sesame and flax seeds.
- Favor lighter grains such as barley or basmati rice.
- Minimize refined sugars; small amounts of honey may be used, but do not cook with it.
- Reduce most nuts; sunflower, pumpkin, flax, or sesame seeds may be taken.
- If you cannot avoid animal products, favor the white meat of turkey or chicken; avoid red meats, particularly pork and beef.
- Drink hot water with sliced or grated fresh ginger frequently throughout the day.
- Do not eat unless you are definitely hungry, and do not overeat.
- Do not eat until the prior meal has been fully digested (three to six hours).

Recipe for Detoxification

A simple-to-prepare detoxifying meal that most people can tolerate for at least a few days is known as *kitchari,* which is a mixture of basmati rice and mung beans.

Ingredients:

This recipe provides four servings.

½ cup whole mung beans (soaked overnight if possible)

1 cup basmati rice

1 tbsp clarified butter (ghee)

½ tsp ground cumin

½ tsp ground coriander

½ tsp ground fennel

½ tsp turmeric

1 tsp salt

4½ cups water

1. Wash the rice in cool water and combine with the soaked mung beans in a 6-quart pot. Add 4½ cups water.
2. Bring the water to a boil, then reduce the heat and cook until most of the water is absorbed (about 30–40 minutes).
3. Melt the clarified butter on low heat in a frying pan and gently roast the spices.
4. Add the spices to the rice and bean mix and continue cooking until the mixture is the consistency of a loose stew.
5. If you desire, you can add chopped vegetables (spinach, zucchini, carrots, and the like), during this last cooking phase.

Deepening the Detoxification

For millennia, Ayurveda has offered a unique and elegant system of detoxification known as *Panchakarma*, usually translated as "purifying actions." The term refers to a process of mobilizing and eliminating toxins from the system, followed by specific rejuvenating procedures. While the full program requires medical supervision for maximal benefits, the basic Chopra Center principles are generally applicable to detoxification.

A unique aspect of this approach is the attention directed to the mobilization and elimination of fat-soluble toxins. The underlying theory is that the substances and patterns that entice us to sacrifice long-term well-being for short-term relief are retained in lipid cell membranes and tissues. In other words the toxins that cause us the most harm are fat-soluble, not water-soluble. Therefore drinking eight cups of water, herbal teas, and fruit juices alone will eliminate only a portion of the toxic ama that inhibits our vitality.

To experience a more profound level of detoxification, you'll need to mobilize and eliminate the fat-soluble toxins that are more deeply buried in your tissues. In promotion of this more intense purification, Ayurveda recommends the ingestion and application of pure, organic herbalized oils. The process is known as "oleation."

The principle of oleation is that through the intake of these organically based lipids, fat-soluble toxins are extracted and eliminated. The oils are employed through two different routes—ingestion and application to the skin. Although traditionally, many different types of oils were prescribed in Ayurveda, we have found that the easiest way to benefit from internal oleation is through the intake of oil-rich seeds.

Flaxseed and sesame seeds have a number of qualities that make them useful in detoxification. Flaxseeds are naturally rich in anti-inflammatory omega-3 fatty acids and hormone-regulating phytoestrogens. They have been shown to lower serum cholesterol levels and inhibit the growth of cancer cells.[1] Flaxseeds are a good source of both soluble and insoluble fiber, which encourage healthy bowel elimination.

Sesame seeds have been prized for thousands of years in Asia and the Middle East. They have natural antibacterial and antiviral properties and have been shown to slow cancer cell growth.[2] Rich in antioxidant and anti-inflammatory properties, sesame seeds are an important source of lignans, natural plant-based chemicals that reduce the risk of breast, prostate, colon, and lung cancer.

In preparation for detoxification, take sesame and flaxseeds for several days prior to the "stop" date. Mix one-quarter cup of raw flaxseeds with one-quarter cup of raw sesame seeds. Heat them together in a skillet until the first seed pops, and then grind the mixture in a coffee bean grinder. Take a tablespoon of the ground seeds four times a day (after each meal and before bed). If you don't have time to prepare this seed mixture yourself, you can obtain similar benefits by taking a teaspoon of tahini (ground sesame seeds) along with a teaspoon of flaxseed oil four times per day. You should notice an overall enhancement in your digestion with improved bowel elimination.

The application of pure oils to the skin is also designed to loosen and mobilize toxins. Beneficial massage oils include sesame seed, almond, olive, coconut, mustard seed, sunflower, and safflower. During your time of detoxification, receiving a daily massage or performing a self-massage facilitates the purification process. This self-massage, known as *abhyanga,* is one of the most important components of the Chopra Center detoxification program.

Full Self-Massage

This entire massage requires just a few tablespoons of warm oil. Begin by massaging your scalp, using small circular strokes as if shampooing your hair. With gentle strokes apply the oil to your forehead, cheeks, and chin, and then move to your ears. Slowly massaging the back of your ears and your temples will have a soothing effect.

Massage a small amount of oil onto the front and back of your neck and then move to your shoulders. When massaging your arms, use circular motions at the shoulders and elbows and long back-and-forth motions on the upper arms and forearms.

Using large, gentle circular motions, massage your chest, stomach, and abdomen. Use an up-and-down motion over your breastbone. Applying a bit of oil to both hands, gently reach around to massage your back and spine as best you can.

As with your arms, massage your legs with a circular motion at the ankles and knees, using a straight back-and-forth motion on the long parts. Use whatever oil remains to massage your feet, paying extra attention to your toes.

Mini-Massage

Your head and feet are the most important parts of your body to massage in preparation for restful sleep. Gently rub a tablespoon of warm oil into your scalp, using the small, circular motions described above. Soothingly massage your forehead from side to side with your palm. Gently massage your temples, then the outside of your ears. Spend a little time massaging the back and front of your neck.

With a second tablespoon of oil, slowly but firmly massage the soles of your feet. Work the oil around your toes with your fingertips. Sit quietly for a few moments to soak in the oil, and then take a warm bath or shower.

Another important component of Panchakarma purification consists of applying heat to the body. There are a number of ways to increase body heat including the ingestion of pungent herbs, immersion in steam baths, herbal wraps, and the application of warm oils. Heating the body liquefies ama and dilates the circulation channels. Sweating induced through heating facilitates the release of toxins.

On the day you begin the process of eliminating a toxic substance or behavior from your life, prepare yourself a hot bath, adding a tablespoon of powdered dry ginger to the water. Soak for ten to fifteen minutes in the tub while envisioning that your body is releasing toxins into the water and that they will soon go down the drain. If you have access to a steam bath, spend a few minutes in it a couple of times during the day, allowing your body to sweat out accumulated toxins. Add a few drops of purifying aromatic oils, such as eucalyptus, juniper, basil, or mint, to the heat source so you can inhale the essential oils while you are sitting in the steam.

Elimination

The traditional Ayurvedic *Panchakarma* literature describes a number of elimination procedures designed to release toxins through the digestive and respiratory tracts. Although most require medical supervision, some procedures can be used safely at home.

To facilitate the release of ama through your digestive system, try a gentle but effective herbal formula known as *Triphala,* which in Sanskrit means "three fruits." Readily available in health food stores, this combination of equal proportions of *Amalaki* (*Emblica officinalis*), *Haritaki* (*Terminalia chebula*), and *Bibhitaki* (*Terminalia belerica*) has been used for thousands of years to encourage healthy elimination from the digestive system. Studies have found that, in addition to its reliable eliminative effects, it has potent antioxidant and immune-restorative properties.[3,4] Along with flax and sesame seeds, Triphala is beneficial in encouraging the removal of energy-blocking ama from the body.

You can try a simple respiratory detoxification process that makes use of a nasal pot, known in Sanskrit as a *neti* pot. This sinus irrigation device, usually made from ceramic or plastic, is filled with warm salt water. Insert the tapered end of the pot gently into one nostril, and while tilting your head to the side, allow the warm saline solution to enter one side and leave the other. Soaking an herbal tea bag containing aromatic spices in the salt water enhances the cleansing effects on the nasal passages. If you are prone to recurrent allergies or sinus infections, a once- or twice-daily sinus cleansing can markedly reduce symptoms.[5] It is common for people withdrawing from addictive substances to experience respiratory congestion, and this gentle procedure can accelerate detoxification, healing, and balance.[6]

Neti Pot

Managing Your Cravings

Even a toxic relationship fulfills some need, so it is common to experience cravings for the old habit, even if most of your mind and body are relieved to have let it go. Cravings are generally worst in the first several days, but may resurface even weeks or months later. It is helpful at these times to remember that you have already been through the most challenging phase of withdrawal, and with a little patience, you can weather the visiting impulse.

It's also helpful to plan in advance how you will handle a temptation. Developing a fail-safe ritual, such as going for a walk, taking a hot bath, going to a yoga class, or calling one of your supportive friends can keep you from relapsing. Recognize the impulse as a wave that will rise and fall. If you can keep breathing through the strongest intensity of the craving, you will notice that it begins to subside and that you can pass the test. With each successful handling of the impulse, you will gain confidence that you can successfully manage your life.

Rejuvenating the Body

Following a detoxification weekend, your cells and tissues are seeking to be replenished through nurturing experiences. Consciously engage in easily digestible sounds, sensations, sights, tastes, and smells to ensure that your agni can metabolize the sensory energy and information into nourishment. Our next chapter explores how to consciously ingest the energy and information of your environment in support of balance, healing, and transformation.

Feeding Your Body, Nourishing Your Mind

As LONG AS SHE could remember, Maria had a confusing relationship with food. As one of six children, she doesn't remember getting much "mom attention" growing up. Despite the perpetual activity in her household, she does remember feeling lonely and using bread and butter sandwiches to soothe her. Inappropriate touching by her oldest brother made her feel confused about her body and the sensations it generated.

As a teenager, she was painfully aware of her size and began what was to be more than a decade of failed attempts to control her weight. From restrictive diets to occasional bouts of bingeing and purging, Maria struggled to find some peace with food. She was attracted to an Ayurvedic approach because she sensed it was more about balance than control, and she desperately needed balance in her life.

At the end of her week at the Chopra Center, where she acquired the tools for a conscious lifestyle, she made three commitments to herself. The first was to take the time to meditate for half an hour twice each day. The second was to begin a consistent exercise program that included yoga, strength training, and cardiovascular exercises. The third was to eat only when her body (not her mind) sent her signals that she was really hungry, and to stop eating when she was comfortably satisfied without being stuffed.

When she returned for a seminar nine months later, she was hardly recognizable, having lost almost thirty pounds. More important, her entire demeanor radiated confidence and poise. She told us that she felt more connected to herself than at any prior time in her life.

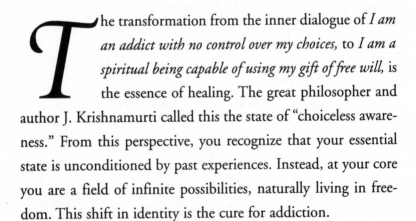

*T*he transformation from the inner dialogue of *I am an addict with no control over my choices,* to *I am a spiritual being capable of using my gift of free will,* is the essence of healing. The great philosopher and author J. Krishnamurti called this the state of "choiceless awareness." From this perspective, you recognize that your essential state is unconditioned by past experiences. Instead, at your core you are a field of infinite possibilities, naturally living in freedom. This shift in identity is the cure for addiction.

You have a body, a mind, and a soul. Your body is a field of molecules woven from the raw material of the environment. Your mind is a field of thoughts, woven from the perceptions and interpretations of your experiences. Your soul is a field of awareness, underlying and giving rise to the subjective reality of your mind and the objective reality of your body. The substance of your body and your mind reflects the quality of the experiences you ingest. This is a core Ayurvedic principle: Experiences are metabolized into biology. A happy mind and vital body are evidence that your experiences have been nourishing you. A distressed mind and depleted body are indications that your perceptions, interpretations, or experiences need to shift.

We perceive the world through our five senses. The sounds we hear, the sensations we feel, the images we see, the foods we taste, and the aromas we smell become the substance of our thoughts and molecules. Although we cannot control every experience we have, we can exercise choice to augment nourishment and minimize toxicity. Let's explore each of the senses to see how we can transform dis-ease into ease.

The Sounds of Sustenance

Human beings are capable of processing auditory information by the second trimester of fetal life. In previous generations we imagined the womb as a quiet place, but we now know that an abundance of sounds and noises filter through the waters of incubation to the unborn child. We begin to hear the people in our lives and the world awaiting us long before we come through the birth canal.

The human ear is capable of perceiving a range of vibrations from 50–20,000 cycles per second. By comparison, dogs, bats, mice, and porpoises can hear sounds above our threshold (ultrasonic sounds), while elephants, baleen whales, and hippopotami can send and receive vibrations well below our range (infrasonic sounds). Of greater significance to our quality of life is the intensity and quality of sound in our environment. The quietest places on Earth, such the Grand Canyon, register ambient noise at about 20 decibels. In the center of an agricultural farm, typical sound levels are 45 decibels. The downtown areas of most major metropolitan cities can average 80 decibels, while a jet plane at takeoff will reach 100 decibels.

Noise pollution has a harmful effect on the health of living beings. Studies have documented that chronic noise toxicity generates emotional tension and anxiety while impairing learning and mental performance. It alters brain neurochemistry, disturbs sleeping patterns, and increases the need for sleeping medications. Chronic noise is associated with high blood pressure and weakened immune function. Sadly, some of the noisiest places on Earth are hospital intensive-care units and emergency departments.

Living in a toxic environment creates distress. Argumentative and hostile voices are among the most toxic sounds to which human beings are exposed. If as a child you were repeatedly exposed to demanding, demeaning, or intimidating sounds, your impulse to fight or escape was activated, generating fear and hostility. But most children are unable to create safety for them-selves. Over time, these threatening voices become internalized, leading to low self-esteem, guilt, and depression. One way to cope with these inner or outer toxic voices is through self-med-ication. The problem, of course, is that once the drugs wear off, the toxic noises return.

Replacing toxic sounds with nourishing ones is essential to healing and transformation. There is a skill in quieting mental turbulence from the past and enhancing the probability of nour-ishing conversations in the future.

Nourishing Sounds

It is as important to ingest healthy sounds as it is to eat healthy foods. Although most of us do not have the opportunity to live in environments that nourish us acoustically around the clock, we can consciously choose to minimize toxic sounds and maximize nurturing sounds in our lives. This involves seeking out and creating pleasing sounds.

The sounds of nature offer the antidote to the noise pollution of modern urban life. We encourage our guests at the Chopra Center to experience places where the only sounds they hear are those of nature—waves crashing against the shore, water rush-ing by in a river, birds making their mating calls. The sounds of nature are primordial. We have been hearing these sounds since the dawn of humanity, and they have the ability to remind us at a visceral level of our ecological connectedness. We encourage you to get a dose of nature's sounds on a regular basis.

Music can be a source of healing vibrations. Music that soothes, relaxes, or inspires influences hormonal levels and physiological activity.[1,2] Music can relieve depressed and anxious moods and reduce pain. It can also boost your immune cells. Music you enjoy generates endorphins, your body's natural pain relievers. When you give people a drug that blocks the effects of narcotics on the brain, they also temporarily lose the ability to experience pleasurable sensations from music.

Music's ability to evoke memories and feelings can change our state of body and mind in a matter of moments. A love song on the radio stirs up reminders of a youthful romance. A rock song from the sixties calls to mind recollections of drug parties in college. A lilting Indian raga may remind you of your summer of freedom spent traveling through Asia.

Poetry, chanting, and singing can all be healing. Pay attention to the toxic sounds you are exposed to and make the commitment to ingest nourishing sounds on a regular basis. Recordings that we find inspiring are listed in the Notes section.[3] Being conscious of the effects of nurturing vibrations will help you substitute life-supporting habits for life-damaging ones.

Nourishing Touch

Mammals require body-to-body contact in order to develop normally. Studies going back decades affirm that loving touch supports physical and emotional development. Baby monkeys who are cuddled by their mothers grow faster and stronger than those whose basic needs for food are met but who are deprived of affection. Rabbits fed a high-cholesterol diet deposit less fat in their blood vessels if they are allowed to cuddle compared to those kept in clean but isolated cages.

Studies on the value of nurturing touch confirm that the skin is a powerful portal into our inner pharmacy.[4-7] We require touch to survive and thrive. Premature babies cuddled and rocked gain weight almost 50 percent faster and are able to go home almost a week earlier than those without tactile stimulation. Touch enhances the production of endorphins, reducing the need for analgesic medication in people recovering from surgery or facing the pain of cancer. Massage has been demonstrated to enhance immune function, improve digestion, reduce agitation in people with Alzheimer's disease, and lower blood pressure.

From the perspective of Ayurveda, the application of pure herbalized oils to the skin encourages the elimination of toxins from the body. During detoxification programs at the Chopra Center for Wellbeing, guests receive daily Ayurvedic treatments utilizing oils infused with purifying and rejuvenating herbs. This *Panchakarma* process is recommended on a seasonal basis as a means of mobilizing ama and keeping the energy channels of circulation open.

As described in Chapter 4, a self-administered massage, abyhanga, is recommended as part of an ideal daily routine. The procedure of abyhanga is a valuable, life-affirming habit to develop. Requiring just a few minutes, it offers benefits throughout the day.

Circulating Affection

Loving touch contributes to our sense of safety. Safety reduces our need to self-medicate with prescription or nonprescription anxiety-reducing chemicals. Make a conscious commitment to touch the people in your life, lovingly and respectfully. Ask for your friends and family members to lovingly embrace you. The soft, warm sensations that are generated when we make contact with another person reflect a cascade of pleasure that generates health-enhancing physiological and biochemical shifts. Be generous with your affection. It benefits you and all those with whom you share your loving touch.

Nourishing Sights

Images of violence incite the physiology of violence. Images of peace engender the physiology of peace. Psychologists at

Harvard University monitored immune function while college students watched films of violence and compassion. Observing images of aggression had no measurable impact on immune function, whereas watching Mother Teresa caring for children resulted in significant enhancement of immune function.[8] Our primitive brains do not easily discriminate between the imaginative display of violence seen in our media and the actual threat of violence. Aggressive images and sounds activate the fight-or-flight response through our involuntary nervous systems. The secretion of stress hormones activates both mind and body into survival mode, even if there is no actual threat to life. This activation contributes to high blood pressure, anxiety, hostility, digestive disturbances, and immune vulnerability. In efforts to calm the psychological and physical turbulence, people are prone to use alcohol or other mind-altering drugs. It is worth remembering: Images of violence beget the physiology of violence.

Images of peace have the opposite effect. Walking through an old-growth forest, watching ocean waves crash upon the shore, observing a hawk riding thermal currents, or appreciating a beautiful garden evoke the physiology of balance and renewal. Peaceful scenes of nature are translated into the physiology of relaxation, which generates the natural chemistry of pleasure and comfort.

Make the conscious choice to experience regular doses of visual nourishment. Take walks though the park. Look up to the sky and allow its vast panorama to expand your mind and your sense of self. Watch entertainment that inspires, amuses, and leaves you feeling enthusiastic about life. Look into the eyes of the people you love, and make a soul-to-soul connection. Use the sense of sight to awaken and remind you of the precious gift of life.

Nourishing Tastes

The human species is the only one on Earth that has turned nutrition into a complicated affair. All other living beings innately recognize the appropriate sources of organic sustenance required for life. Bengal tigers do not attend conferences that debate the latest research on the appropriate balance of omega-3 and omega-6 fatty acids to reduce heart disease. Termites do not subscribe to magazines that promote the nutritional value of a particular brand of wood over another. Only people have such a challenging affair with food.

From the perspective of Ayurveda, healthy nutrition doesn't need to be so complicated. Like every other living species, our bodies know what they need to maintain optimal health. Ideal nutrition derives from simple principles that reflect basic aspects of our physiology. It has been our experience that once you understand these simple tenets, you'll never need to struggle with your diet again.

Underlying the dimension of physical reality that is accessible to our senses is a field of energy and information. From this point of view we can see our bodies as constellations of energy and information composed of matter and energy derived from our environment. Eating is the process of converting the energy and information of our environment into the energy and information of our bodies. An apple is a package of energy and information. Digestion is the process of transforming the energy and information of the apple into the energy and information of our body. Balanced input translates into a healthy physiology.

Six Codes of Ingestible Intelligence

Ayurveda addressed the question of healthy nutrition over five millennia ago by asking, "How do we know what to eat?" The answer that has served the test of time is, "Listen to your body." Human beings are capable of discriminating six different flavors of food, which represent the major sources of nutrition we require. These six tastes are:

Sweet • Sour • Savory • Pungent • Bitter • Astringent

SWEET

Sweet foods are those rich in energy, which we measure scientifically as calories. Foods in the sweet category are those abundant in carbohydrates, proteins, and fats. Examples of sweet foods include: grains, pasta, breads, nuts, dairy, oils, sweet fruits, starchy vegetables, fish, poultry, meat, and sugar. A healthy diet favors complex carbohydrates, sweet fruits, vegetable sources of protein, and low-fat dairy, while reducing highly refined carbohydrates and red meat. To satisfy your sweet flavor needs in a healthy way, favor whole grains, nuts and seeds, fresh fruits, and organic low-fat dairy. Gently reduce your consumption of highly refined carbohydrates, and see if you can gradually wean yourself from red meats in favor of chicken, fish, and vegetable protein sources.

SOUR

Sour is the taste of acid, which our bodies require to perform many vital functions ranging from optimal digestion to infection-fighting inflammation. Examples of foods containing organic acids that generate the sour taste include citrus fruits, berries, tomatoes, tart fruits, vinegar, chutneys, salad dressings, pickles, condiments, and alcohol. Natural sources of sour are preferable to those that derive their sour taste from fermentation.

SAVORY

Savory is the taste of the ocean. Every land-dwelling animal once had to internalize the primordial ocean soup by developing a circulatory system. In fact the saline content of our blood is very similar to that of the primordial ocean. On a daily basis we must replenish the salt we lose through our perspiration and elimination. In the past, landlocked communities struggled to receive adequate salt in their diet; yet we are at greater risk in modern societies of ingesting too much, rather than not enough, salt. Sources of the savory flavor include table salt, fish, meat, seaweed, soy sauce, and many processed and canned foods. Although we clearly need salt in our diet, reducing our intake of processed foods will ensure that we avoid overdosing on it.

PUNGENT

The pungent taste in spicy foods derives from essential oils that stimulate the tongue and mucous membranes of the mouth. Pungent foods are digestive stimulants and naturally detoxifying. Most are rich in healthy antioxidants as well. Examples of pungent foods include pepper, cayenne, ginger, garlic, onions, leeks, chilies, radish, horseradish, salsa, and cloves. Many green herbs such as basil, thyme, oregano, and rosemary are mild to moderately spicy. Getting regular doses of pungent foods contributes to healthy digestion and enhanced immunity.

BITTER

Bitter is the taste of vegetables, particularly green leafy vegetables. Foods that carry a bitter taste are naturally detoxifying and rich in nutrients necessary for healthy physiological function. Spinach, chard, kale, zucchini, string beans, asparagus, and Brussels sprouts are examples of predominantly bitter foods. Many medicinal herbs carry the bitter taste.

Many organic chemicals contained in vegetables have potent antioxidant and natural cancer-fighting properties. Numerous

studies have demonstrated the health benefits of five to nine help-
ings of vegetables and fruits each day, but less than 25 percent of
people take advantage of nature's health-promoting pharmacy. As
you commit to transforming unhealthy habits into healthy ones,
include detoxifying foods with bitter tastes in your diet.

ASTRINGENT

Astringent foods have a healing effect on the body. Their
place in Western nutrition has diminished over the past century
to the detriment of our health. Foods in this category offer
important nutritional value. The astringent flavor is available
most abundantly in legumes, beans, peas, and lentils. It is also
found in tea, cranberries, pomegranates, and fresh spinach.

There are many health benefits that derive from astringent
foods. Legumes provide good sources of vegetable protein and
fiber. Beans contain natural hormone-balancing chemicals that
have been shown to reduce the risk of a number of cancers.

Ingesting Light

Healthy foods offer a practical way to bring light into your
body to dispel the darkness of toxicity. All food is ultimately
transformed sunlight, but the typical Western diet is predominantly shades of white and brown (meat, dairy, cereal grains,
potatoes). Bringing in a wide spectrum of light to your body is
purifying and healing.

Make an effort to consciously introduce naturally colorful foods into your diet. Red tomatoes, watermelon, and red grapefruit carry lycopene, a natural cancer-fighting chemical. The orange color of carrots and tangerines carry potent health-promoting antioxidants. Bananas and yellow peppers offer beneficial doses of vitamin A, potassium, and fiber. Green leafy vegetables are concentrated sources of detoxifying antioxidant molecules. The blues and purples of berries, cherries, and grapes are rich in natural substances called anthocyanins. These are some of the most potent antioxidants, which have been correlated with lower risks for heart disease and enhanced immunity. Nature provides us an effective healing pharmacy in the form of fruits, vegetables, beans, and grains. Expand your intake of nourishment through the tastes and colors of nature, and your mind and body will reward you with reduced cravings for those things that provide momentary relief but fail to serve your deeper needs.

"Light" Foods
Include in Your Diet Several Times a Day

Foods	Natural Health-Promoting Chemicals	Benefits
Tomatoes, red grapefruit, watermelon, guavas	Lycopene	Anti-cancer Antioxidant
Berries, cherries, grapes	Anthocyanins	Antioxidant, Strengthen immunity
Broccoli, grapes, apples, citrus fruits, cherries, berries	Flavonoids	Antioxidant, Protect against heart disease
Tree nuts, berries, apples, grapes, plums, apricots	Phenolic compounds	Antioxidant Anti-cancer
Broccoli, cauliflower, Brussels sprouts, cabbage	Isothiocyanates	Antioxidant Anti-cancer
Cinnamon, rosemary, thyme, turmeric	Terpenoids	Antioxidant Antibacterial Digestion strengthening

Nourishing Aromas

As human beings, we may not be as conscious of the sense of smell as of our other senses, but it is no less important. The part of our brain that processes smell is intimately connected with our emotions, our memories, and our primitive reactions. Most

animals use the sense of smell to make their most critical decisions such as identifying their enemies, food sources, and mates.
As people our threshold for noticing aromatic stimulus is higher
than for sight or sound, but olfactory information is continually
registering and being processed. Remember a time when you
realized you had overbaked cookies in the oven. It was too late
to salvage them by the time you recognized the smell, but in fact
you were aware of the odor long before it registered in your
awareness. Smell is a powerful sense that influences us in a predominantly subliminal way.

Studies have shown that newborn babies recognize and prefer
their own mother's smells to other women's scent. The fragrance
of your lover's signature cologne may evoke memories, fantasies,
and rapture while you are in the relationship, but may elicit
anguish or revulsion after the relationship has ended. The aroma
of cinnamon buns or espresso may provoke feelings of pleasure
or distress depending upon whether you are in a mind-set to
indulge or struggling to abstain. If you are in the withdrawal
stage of breaking a habit, the scent of a cigarette may trigger
intense cravings, whereas a year later the same smell may be
repulsive. Real estate agents bake bread in the oven of a house
that is languishing on the market in the hopes that potential
buyers will subconsciously associate the smell with fantasies
about a safe, nurturing home for their family.

Recognizing the power of aroma, we can use smell to awaken
healing and balance. Natural fragrances have intrinsic properties

based upon the source of the aromatic molecules. In general the essential oils of herbs, spices, flowers, and fruits have physiological properties similar to the botanical substances from which they derive. The fragrance of stimulating plants tends to be stimulating. The aroma of soothing or sedating plants tends to be calming.

Lavender, cedarwood, ylang ylang, and bergamot have a relaxing effect on the mind and can be used to quiet anxiety and treat insomnia. Juniper, peppermint, and rosemary have invigorating effects and are helpful to relieve mental and physical fatigue. Jasmine, sandalwood, and rose oils have a pacifying influence, which can help soothe irritation. Many studies on aromatherapy have suggested that living beings respond in predictable ways to the inhalation of essential oils.[9-11]

In addition to the direct physiological effects of aromatherapy, you can use essential oils to evoke a desired conditioned response. As you are transitioning from a physiology that is wrapped around an addiction, find those experiences that bring you healthy pleasures and associate them with a pleasing aroma. Ask your massage therapist to use lavender oil while giving you a treatment so your brain associates the fragrance with the experience of enjoyable relaxation. Have sandalwood essential oil perfusing in your room while you are practicing yoga or meditation so you make the connection between the aroma and a quiet mind. Then use the fragrances at other times when you are feeling anxious to still the voice that begins calling you to indulge in the old behavior you are committed to extinguishing.

Conscious Choice Making

The challenge addiction presents is finding nourishing substitutions to fulfill your deep underlying needs for love, self-esteem, safety, and meaning in your life. Once you understand that your experiences are metabolized into the substance of your mind and body, you can begin making conscious choices to transform your experiences so you can transform your life. Your sensory experiences are the portals to your inner pharmacy. Use them to awaken the natural chemistry of health and happiness.

Awakening Your Energy

PUSHING TO MEET DEADLINES at his public relations company, Alex found the demands of his job exceeded his body's endurance. Even though he was practically irrigating his brain with caffeine, he found his attention fading in the evening hours when he needed to stay focused. A coworker suggested he try one of his Adderall tablets, a prescription medication comprising four amphetamine salts used for attention deficit disorder.

Alex liked the alertness and concentration he felt on the drug, but didn't like the occasional rapid heartbeat, restlessness, or headaches he was experiencing. He was particularly concerned that even though he felt groggy once the effects wore off, he didn't sleep well at night. Without deeply resting at night, he felt sluggish the next day, and this lethargy prompted him to take more drugs. Alex was aware he was trapped in a cycle.

Our conventional biomedical model views human beings as molecular machines. As science continues working out the details, biologists anticipate that we will fully understand life by looking at the biochemical reactions that underlie metabolism and reproduction. From this point of view, whenever there is a problem with a person's mind or body, it is reducible to the underlying molecules. It then follows that the most effective intervention is the introduction of new molecules developed in a pharmaceutical laboratory. Your heartburn is the result of too many hydrochloric acid molecules, so a prescription for an acid blocker should take care of the problem. Your insomnia is the consequence of too few gamma-amino-butyric acid (GABA) molecules, so a dose of a GABA-activating medicine should put you to sleep. Your depression and fatigue are caused by an inadequate concentration of serotonin molecules, so taking a selective serotonin reuptake inhibitor (SSRI) will improve your mood and disposition.

Western medicine has a most effective approach to relieving the symptoms of illness but rarely addresses the underlying emotional or lifestyle issues that fuel the problems. The consideration that patients' digestive disturbances, insomnia, or exhaustion are related to choices they have made, or are making, is given little attention. The problem with Western medicine, lamented Mahatma Gandhi, is that it is so good at treating the symptoms of illness that people are not motivated to look at what they are doing that contributes to their distress.

Eastern health systems including Traditional Chinese Medicine and Ayurveda recognize the physical expression of illness but call upon us to explore the conditions that enable disease to arise. Within this context, illness is seen as a blockage or stagnation of vital energy. Health is the expression of the life force flowing freely.

This life force is known in Traditional Chinese Medicine as *chi*, which flows through meridians in the body. In Ayurveda this vital energy, which circulates through channels known as *nadis*, goes by the name *prana*. When prana is blocked, our sense of wholeness is disrupted, and we experience anxiety, depression, fatigue, and pain. Life energy purifies and nourishes every aspect of our minds and bodies. When it is not able to circulate freely, we lose our natural ability to maintain balance and generate natural comfort. In the quest to regain balance and reduce discomfort, people may engage in habitual behaviors that provide momentary relief but fail to address the underlying causes and ultimately contribute to further distress.

Conscious Energy Management

In addition to regular meditation, a healthy diet, and nourishing sensory input, your thoughts and actions influence the quality of life energy circulating in your mind and body. When attempting to eliminate a life-harming habit, one of the most important behaviors you can introduce into your life is a daily practice that encourages balance, flexibility, and centered awareness. This daily practice helps to decongest the channels of circulation, enhance vitality, reduce stress, and generate natural pleasure-inducing chemicals.

Yoga, the ancient system of conscious movement from India, remains one of the most effective methods for enhancing flexibility and balance. Although often viewed in the West as a system for physically stretching the body, the intention of yoga is much deeper than that. The essence of yoga is a technology for quieting the mind and cultivating a state of body-centered restful awareness. Yoga is designed to integrate the physical, emotional, and spiritual aspects of an individual so life energy can move freely throughout the body.

In the classical literature of yoga, eight different dimensions are addressed to awaken the memory of wholeness. These are sometimes referred to as the eight limbs of yoga, known in Sanskrit as *Yama, Niyama, Asana, Pranayama, Pratyahara, Dharana, Dhyana,* and *Samadhi.* Each of these aspects has some insight to offer as you move from a constricted sense of self to a more expanded one.

Freeing Your Energy—Yamas and Niyamas

The *Yamas* represent the codes of behavior that support the free flow of energy. We are encouraged to live impeccably, not because a Santa-like deity sits in judgment of our choices, but because we wish to minimize actions that generate unnecessary friction. The bottom line for these rules of engagement is to behave toward others as if they were reflections of ourselves.

The *Niyamas* describe the inner dialogue of people dedicated to the impeccable management of their life energy. Ruminations about past regrets or anxieties about future possibilities deplete vital energy and inhibit us from living with awareness in the present. Remaining centered and focused on the next choice enables us to digest what is happening now and extract maximal value from it.

Asana

Asana means seat or posture. This is what people typically associate with the word "yoga"—the positions that enhance flexibility in the body. The popularity of yoga in the West is a testament to its noticeable benefits on well-being. From a yogic perspective, asanas awaken mental and physical vitality because they enhance the flow of life energy throughout the body. There are hundreds of different postures that can awaken healing and transformation in physiological systems, and people benefit from an asana practice throughout their lives.

Sun Salutations

The foundation of an asana practice is a set of twelve poses known as *Surya Namaskar*, or Sun Salutations. This sequence of poses stretches and tones all major muscle groups and spontaneously supports the movement of energy through the body. They also gently massage your internal organs. As you are casting off negative behaviors and favoring life-supporting ones, we strongly encourage you to integrate the Sun Salutations into your daily routine.

FIRST POSTURE: SALUTATION POSE

Stand with your feet on the ground and your hands together at your chest. Center your awareness in your body, breathing easily.

SECOND POSTURE: SKY-REACHING POSE

Reach toward the sky with both hands, stretching up through your shoulders, back, and chest. Slowly inhale while elongating your body.

THIRD POSTURE: HAND-TO-FEET POSE

Gently stretch forward while placing your hands on the outsides of your feet. Bend your knees if you need to, while exhaling.

READER/CUSTOMER CARE SURVEY

HEFG

We care about your opinions! Please take a moment to fill out our online Reader Survey at **http://survey.hcibooks.com.**
As a **"THANK YOU"** you will receive a **VALUABLE INSTANT COUPON** towards future book purchases
as well as a **SPECIAL GIFT** available only online! Or, you may mail this card back to us.

(PLEASE PRINT IN ALL CAPS)

First Name _____ MI. _____ Last Name _____

Address _____

State _____ Zip _____ City _____ Email _____

1. Gender
- ☐ Female
- ☐ Male

2. Age
- ☐ 8 or younger
- ☐ 9-12
- ☐ 13-16
- ☐ 17-20
- ☐ 21-30
- ☐ 31+

3. Did you receive this book as a gift?
- ☐ Yes
- ☐ No

4. Annual Household Income
- ☐ under $25,000
- ☐ $25,000 - $34,999
- ☐ $35,000 - $49,999
- ☐ $50,000 - $74,999
- ☐ over $75,000

5. What are the ages of the children living in your house?
- ☐ 0 - 14
- ☐ 15+

6. Marital Status
- ☐ Single
- ☐ Married
- ☐ Divorced
- ☐ Widowed

7. How did you find out about the book?
(please choose one)
- ☐ Recommendation
- ☐ Store Display
- ☐ Online
- ☐ Catalog/Mailing
- ☐ Interview/Review

8. Where do you usually buy books?
(please choose one)
- ☐ Bookstore
- ☐ Online
- ☐ Book Club/Mail Order
- ☐ Price Club (Sam's Club, Costco's, etc.)
- ☐ Retail Store (Target, Wal-Mart, etc.)

9. What subject do you enjoy reading about the most?
(please choose one)
- ☐ Parenting/Family
- ☐ Relationships
- ☐ Recovery/Addictions
- ☐ Health/Nutrition
- ☐ Christianity
- ☐ Spirituality/Inspiration
- ☐ Business Self-help
- ☐ Women's Issues
- ☐ Sports

10. What attracts you most to a book?
(please choose one)
- ☐ Title
- ☐ Cover Design
- ☐ Author
- ☐ Content

TAPE IN MIDDLE; DO NOT STAPLE

‖‖‖

BUSINESS REPLY MAIL
FIRST-CLASS MAIL PERMIT NO 45 DEERFIELD BEACH, FL

POSTAGE WILL BE PAID BY ADDRESSEE

Health Communications, Inc.
3201 SW 15th Street
Deerfield Beach FL 33442-9875

ɪ.ɪɪ.ɪɪ.ɪɪɪ.ɪ.ɪ.ɪ.ɪ.ɪ.ɪ.ɪ.ɪɪ.ɪ.ɪɪ.ɪ.ɪ.ɪ.ɪ.ɪ.ɪɪ.ɪɪ.ɪ.ɪ.ɪ.ɪ.ɪ

FOLD HERE

Comments

FOURTH POSTURE: EQUESTRIAN POSE

Stretch back your left leg while bending at the right knee.
Breathe easily in this equestrian pose, feeling a gentle stretch in
your neck and upper back.

FIFTH POSTURE: MOUNTAIN POSE

Bringing your left foot back to your right, move into the mountain pose by raising your buttocks into the air. Flexing your chin toward your chest, feel the stretch through your arms and legs.

SIXTH POSTURE: EIGHT LIMBS POSE

Lower yourself into the eight limbs pose, just touching your forehead, chest, and knees to the floor. Most of your weight is borne on your hands and toes, as if at the bottom of a pushup.

SEVENTH POSTURE: COBRA POSE

Moving into the cobra pose, lift your chest off the ground, mainly using your back and chest muscles. Be careful not to push too hard with your hands to avoid straining your back. Inhale as you move into this extension pose.

EIGHTH POSTURE: MOUNTAIN POSE

During the second half of the cycle, you retrace the postures performed in the first half. As you exhale, lift your hips and buttocks, stretching through your arms and legs.

NINTH POSTURE: EQUESTRIAN POSE

In the second equestrian pose, bring your right leg back, while bending the left leg. Inhale as you move into this position.

TENTH POSTURE: HAND-TO-FEET POSE

Bringing your feet together, bend forward at the hips. Exhale as you place your hands along the sides of your feet.

ELEVENTH POSTURE: SKY-REACHING POSE

Inhaling, unfold your spine, reaching upward to the sky. Feel the stretch through your arms, neck, and spine.

TWELFTH POSTURE: SALUTATION POSE

To complete the cycle, return to the salutation pose with hands together at the level of your heart, breathing easily. With your eyes closed, notice the sensation of energy in your body and the easy flow of your breath.

Performed slowly with awareness, the Sun Salutations are meditative. They can be performed more vigorously to provide a cardiovascular workout. Begin with a few sets and gradually increase the number of rounds you perform, always staying in tune with your breath. The basic principle is to inhale with every posture of extension and exhale with each flexion. Allow each pose to flow smoothly into the next for maximal benefit. The Sun Salutations cultivate flexibility in body and mind.

Regulating Your Life Force—*Pranayama*

Pranayama means regulation of the life force. Since the breath is so intimately associated with vital energy, *pranayama* usually refers to breathing exercises that consciously calm or invigorate one's mind and body. Breathing is one of the few physiological processes that we can easily influence through conscious intention, but it usually flows without having to think about it. By bringing attention to our breathing, we can change the quality and quantity of vital energy.

There are a number of different *pranayama* breathing exercises that can be useful in focusing the mind and rejuvenating the body. We'll review three of the most important ones here.

The first has a calming, settling effect on the mind and body and can help to relieve anxiety and insomnia. The second is invigorating and useful when you want to promptly change your mood or mind-set. The third has a clearing influence on the body and helps create body-centered restful awareness.

Alternate Nostril Breathing—
Nadi Shodhana

Nadi Shodhana means purifying the circulatory channels. It is commonly referred to in English as alternate nostril breathing. As a gentle, calming breathing exercise, Nadi Shodhana has a soothing, harmonizing effect on the physiology. When your mind is racing and you are consumed with turbulent thoughts about what has or might transpire, practice a few minutes of this breathing exercise and notice its centering influence.

The easiest way to perform this breathing practice is by alternately closing off a nostril at the end of each inhalation. Using your right thumb, compress your right nostril after you have taken a slow full breath. Next, exhale slowly and fully through your left nostril and then inhale through the same left nostril. At the peak of inhalation, compress the left nostril using your third and fourth fingers, and exhale fully through the right nostril. At the end of your exhalation, breathe in through the same right nostril until you have reached the peak of inhalation. Then repeat the cycle, closing the right nostril and exhaling through the left.

Continue rhythmically breathing for about three to five minutes. As you feel quieter, you may close your eyes, simply allowing your awareness to be with your breath.

Bellows Breath—Bhastrika

Bhastrika is controlled hyperventilation. Both the inhalation and exhalation are through the nose, using the diaphragm to move air in and out of the lungs. When you find yourself feeling agitated, acting irritable, or craving something to change your state, perform a few rounds of Bhastrika. The rapid shifts in blood chemistry generated with this breathing can quickly transform the quality and content of your thoughts.

Sitting comfortably, begin slow, deep breathing through your nose. After a few slow breaths, begin the Bellows Breath practice by generating forceful full exhalations followed by forceful full inhalations. This should be at the rate of approximately one per second. Try keeping your head and shoulders relaxed and stable, allowing all air movement to flow from abdominal breathing.

Perform ten to fifteen deep, rapid nasal breaths and then relax into normal breathing. Wait about ten seconds and then repeat another cycle of ten to fifteen breaths. Perform a few sets when you first begin this practice, gradually increasing to ten cycles once you are comfortable. Although Bhastrika is generally safe, if you begin to feel uncomfortably light-headed, stop the forceful breathing until the sensation passes. It's best to avoid this exercise if you are pregnant. This breathing practice is designed to create a sense of clarity and invigoration.

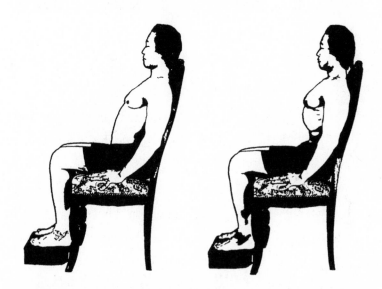

Complete Breath—Dirgha Breath

This breathing exercise has a balancing and purifying effect on mind and body. It can be performed either sitting or lying down. The process consists of sequentially filling your lungs from bottom to top, while inhaling through the nose.

Begin the exercise by slowing inhaling while directing air into the lower spaces of your lungs. As you begin the practice, your belly should expand as if you were pregnant. Practice this several times until you are comfortable bringing air into the lower part of your lungs.

The second step involves directing air to the middle chambers of your lungs. First, fill the lower section and then continue inhaling as you move air into the central spaces. As you are doing this, you will feel your chest expanding.

The final step begins by slowly filling the lower and middle parts of your lungs and then continuing to inhale into the upper regions. Imagine you are bringing air into your collarbones. Through this process, you are filling your entire lungs. Practice this complete breath several times.

While exhaling, reverse the process, first emptying the upper chambers, then the middle, and then the lower. Your smooth and flowing inhalations and exhalations encourage the efficient and effortless flow of energy throughout your body.

The Final Four Limbs of Yoga— Pratyahara, Dharana, Dhyana, Samadhi

The last four limbs of yoga encourage the inward direction of attention. We discussed Pratyahara in Chapter 4 on detoxification in the context of simplifying your sensory experience so you can fully metabolize what you have already ingested. Closing your eyes and temporarily disengaging from the world of form and phenomena help organize and clarify your life.

Dharana describes the first principle of meditation in which we direct our attention from the outer to the inner world. Dhyana (from which the word "Zen" is derived) refers to the process of witnessing the flow of thoughts in the mind without engaging in resistance or anticipation. This enables us to choose our emotional responses rather than reacting as conditioned beings. Finally, Samadhi is the state of union experienced when the mind is quiet and the body is deeply relaxed. In this state all desires find their fulfillment. Tapping into this experience on a daily basis through meditation renews and energizes our body, mind, and soul. It is the ultimate realization of all addictive behaviors—an internally generated state of peace, happiness, harmony, and love.

Energy-Efficient Living

Life energy is our most precious commodity. Used wisely it empowers all our intentions and ensures a life of creativity and freedom. Our experience at the Chopra Center convinces us that people willing to replace energy-squandering habits with energy-awakening ones stop making life-damaging choices. Make the commitment to add yoga poses, conscious breathing practices, and meditation to your life for six weeks, and notice how your thoughts, feelings, and experience of yourself and the world transform.

Emotional Emancipation

SAM WAS TIRED OF riding the emotional energy roller coaster. His cups of coffee which charged him up throughout the day at work made it difficult for him to turn his mind off in the evening. He had developed the habit of breaking open a bottle of wine immediately upon arriving home, and it was not uncommon for him to finish it off by the time he went to bed. He did not like the path he saw himself on, and he knew that he needed to create more balance in his life.

Given his childhood in which he moved numerous times between the households of his divorced parents, it was not surprising that Sam had trouble remembering times when he felt safe in his body. In his quest for emotional balance, he was committed to identifying and digesting his accumulated emotional toxicity through a holistic mind-body approach.

*M*aintaining the boundaries of your individuality can be, at times, a daunting task. Your core expectations are simple. You want unconditional love and acceptance. You want nourishing attention, affection, and appreciation. You want effortless abundance, frictionless relationships, a deep connection to your core meaning and purpose, and an unassailable sense of freedom. Simple.

You have these intentions and desires because at some faint level of awareness you remember a state of being in which these experiences were reality. Perhaps it was as a young child when your days were spent reveling in the moment without a care for what the next day might bring. Perhaps there are the subtle remembrances of your intrauterine experience where every need was instantaneously met. Perhaps we all carry the seeds of memory from a pre-incarnated state in which some aspect of our being floated freely beyond time or space.

However these core expectations for unconditional happiness are created, they are not met for most people in a sustainable manner. Mothers and caregivers do their best to fulfill the needs of a baby, but at times, their capacity to attend to every demand is exceeded, and babies experience the distress of unmet needs. We have a built-in mechanism to demonstrate our dissatisfaction when the universe fails to acknowledge our central place in it: We wail. Crying, howling, and throwing tantrums may get the attention of those capable of fulfilling our wants, but at some point we discover that these energy-expending expressions are inconsistently effective and may actually have the opposite effect of distancing the very people we are trying to attract.

Along the way, we learn that performing in ways that please our caregivers may bring us the attention and affection we seek. Smiling on request, toddling over to Mama, and repeating new words yield enthusiastic cheers and applause. Very early on we begin honing the lifelong process of balancing our desire for autonomy with our dependence on others to provide us what we need.

Deciphering Expectations

Long before we consciously understood the rules, we learned that we are rewarded when we meet the expectations of our parents, caregivers, and teachers, and punished when we don't. The reprimand may be gentle, as when we go potty in our pants instead of asking to go to the toilet, or harsh when we chase a ball into the street. Through more or less subtle feedback, we strive, struggle, and learn to navigate our unique paths to internal comfort.

Consider the messages you received growing up. If your parents were professors, engineers, or doctors, any aptitude you showed in science, math, or academic accomplishment probably elicited gestures of approval. If a parent was an artist or musician, your expression of artistic talent may have been reinforced with praise and encouragement. If athletic prowess was esteemed in your household, your sports achievements were highly prized.

If your innate talents aligned with the values of your caregivers, the early trajectory of your life may have been comparatively easy to establish. However, if your nature was not in harmony with what was valued in your home, it is likely you experienced this discord in your mind and body. The goal for every human is a state of inner comfort. If we cannot have total bliss, we'll negotiate for the best possible substitute.

This dance between children and parents rarely occurs on a conscious level. The expectations of our caregivers are usually conveyed through subtle rewards and punishments. If as a child you were not comfortable with the terms for approval, acceptance, and appreciation, you had a limited repertoire of ways to express your dissatisfaction. When the approval you were seeking was not forthcoming, you demonstrated your discomfort either by acting out or drawing inward. Expressed outwardly, you may have whined, complained, yelled, or thrown a tantrum. Internalized, you may have pouted, withdrawn, or made yourself physically sick. Sadly, these primitive demonstrations were often unsuccessful in getting your needs met, and may have had the unintended consequence of pushing your caregivers away.

We survive this process by creating a personality. We hone our thoughts, words, body language, and actions to maximize inner comfort and minimize distress. We identify with those beliefs, preferences, and behaviors we believe are the most likely to provide a self-image we can feel good about. If the symbols with which we wove our identity feel comfortable as we grow, we develop a healthy self-image. If the traits we acquired to get our basic needs met as children do not serve us as adults, we experience emotional turmoil.

Feeling Relief Through Self-Medication

We see many people struggling with addictive behaviors that developed in response to early conflicts between their parents and themselves. Parents may have been remote and unavailable, and the habit developed to soothe feelings of abandonment. Parents may have been overly controlling, and the habitual behavior may have served as an act of rebellion or as an effort to relieve the distress arising from too little personal freedom. If someone discovered that drinking a six-pack of beer, smoking a joint, or taking speed gave them temporary reprieve from their life conflicts, they repeated that behavior and became dependent upon it.

Unfortunately, most addictive behaviors provide diminishing relief over time, but people persist in the habit because it has become woven into their psychological and physical fabrics. Although drugs may provide transient reduction in distress, they usually don't make any contribution to resolving the underlying conflict. Getting drunk doesn't make your mother more available or your father less critical. It may anesthetize you for a short time, but as the chemical wears off, the underlying pain resurfaces.

EMOTIONAL HEALING ————————————

We can't do anything to change the past except to reinterpret it. We can, however, release the accumulated pain that drives life-damaging choices. Like the physical detoxification program we discussed in Chapter 4, we have developed an emotional detoxification process that helps free people from the psychological burdens they've been carrying. The principles that support genuine and lasting emotional healing are similar to those that apply to physical healing.

If a person has a bacterial infection but doesn't have sufficient immune response to eliminate it, the immune system does its best to wall off the infection in abscesses. The contained infection then smolders in capsules of containment, neither fully resolving nor killing the host, yet draining the life energy of the person. Similarly, we wall off emotional abscesses that smolder in our hearts and drain our vitality. Just as we must release physical toxins in order for our bodies to be healthy, we must drain emotional toxins for our hearts to be healthy.

FOUR STEPS TO EMOTIONAL DETOXIFICATION ——

To eliminate something that is blocking the free flow of energy in mind and body, you must first acknowledge that it exists and identify what it is. The most direct way of identifying emotional toxicity is listening to your heart and feeling your body. Try this simple exercise now.

EMOTIONAL DETOX STEP ONE: ACKNOWLEDGE YOUR EMOTIONS

Take a deep breath, hold it for about a count of ten, and then release it slowly. Close your eyes, center your attention in your heart, and allow yourself to feel the sensations residing there. Pay attention to any feelings of constriction, sadness, anger, or frustration. Notice if you sense anxiety, grief, guilt, or hostility. Allow yourself to feel the sensations residing in your heart without resistance. Rather than struggling against them, surrender into them. Immerse yourself in the feelings, breathing into them as you might remind yourself not to hold your breath while you are at the dentist. After five or ten minutes of identifying the feelings residing in your heart, you are ready for the next step.

EMOTIONAL DETOX STEP TWO: MOBILIZE EMOTIONAL TOXICITY

Emotional pain may be buried deep in the mind and heart, but it will continue to drain your vital energy. The psychological energy invested in suppressing and repressing emotional pain predisposes us to depression. The mechanism to release the stored pain is to access the feelings and memories that are trapped and move them through awareness. This, in fact, is the basis of professional counseling, and it is often beneficial, if not essential, to create a relationship with a therapist who is familiar with the dynamics of addiction and the underlying emotional issues that contribute to uncomfortable feelings and the behaviors that numb them.

At the Chopra Center, we have found that journaling is a useful way to mobilize toxic emotions. A number of scientific studies also support the role of journaling on mental and physical health. Giving yourself permission to acknowledge and express in writing the painful experiences that you've locked inside is emotionally liberating.

Start by making a list of the people in your life with whom you associate pain and disappointment. Begin with the most recent relationships and continue thinking your way back throughout the course of your life. Your list may look something like this:

> *Recent partner who had an affair*
> *Ex-spouse who treated me abusively*
> *College roommate who slept with my lover*
> *Athletics teacher in high school who spoke disparagingly to me*
> *Older sibling who was mean to me*
> *Parent who was emotionally absent from my life*

Once you've compiled your list of people, begin addressing experiences. If you had a long-term relationship with someone, you will have many individual memories in which your needs were not met, resulting in emotional distress. Take the time to chronicle each episode that surfaces in your awareness. If you make a genuine commitment to this process, memories of events will pop into your awareness at unexpected times. You may have dreams about situations you had long ago consciously forgotten. You may be watching television or a movie and suddenly recall something that you had not considered in years. Indeed you'll know that this method of draining these toxic emotions is working when you are "surprised" by memories. It is as if your subconscious mind recognizes and relishes the opportunity to release emotional pain.

As you process the emotional information that you have accessed, consider the memorable experience from the perspective of what happened and what you felt. As you replay painful experiences from your past, emotional energy will be released. Feelings of sadness, disappointment, hopelessness, anger, loneliness, and fear reflect the mobilization of toxic emotions. Do not resist the emergence of these strong feelings, even though they may be uncomfortable. Allow yourself to feel the sensations without resistance or anticipation. Let the feelings wash over you, trusting that their movement is an expression of healing.

EMOTIONAL DETOX STEP THREE: RELEASE EMOTIONAL TOXICITY

Rituals have powerful emotional and physical effects. They capture our attention and serve as milestones in life. Baptisms, birthday parties, communions, confirmations, graduations, weddings, holidays, and funerals all serve as declarations of chapter beginnings and endings in the book of life. If you are ready to close the chapter in your story that keeps you engaging in life-damaging behaviors, a ritual of emotional release can be powerful and liberating.

Having stirred up your emotional pain through journaling your history of relationships and experiences that created distress, a releasing exercise is designed to move the toxic feelings out of your body. Begin by reviewing your journal writings, highlighting the core issues that anchor your emotional suffering. As you read what you have written, capture the nucleus of the pain with a word or short phrase. For example, if you have memories of your mother being unavailable for extended periods of time, resulting in feelings of not being worthy of love, write down *unlovable*. If your alcoholic father regularly projected his self-loathing onto you, write down *abusive fathering*. In Eastern philosophical traditions, this principle is known as *sutra* practice. A sutra is a "stitch" that holds together ideas. The English words "suture" and "ligature" are derived from sutra. As you are working through this process, you want to identify the sutras that are holding your pain together—the words for the feelings and beliefs that continue to generate emotional distress. A partial list may look like the following:

Unlovable messages from mother
Abusive critical fathering
Frequently called "fat" by adolescent friends
Sexually objectified by first husband—unable to set healthy boundaries
Weak-willed in subsequent relationships
Betrayed by unscrupulous business partner
Ongoing subtle emotional abuse by current spouse

Each of these short phrases represents patterns of experience that have created distress. The phrase is the suture that holds the painful thought loop together. The value of this process is getting all the painful emotional tapes in one box in preparation for dumping them. Although it can seem at times as if the burden of emotional toxicity is unlimited, this step is designed to get your mind around the issues so you can free yourself from their constricting influence.

EMOTIONAL DETOX STEP FOUR:
YOUR PILGRIMAGE TO FREEDOM

Once you have your list of sutras, take a trip to a place where you can release your feelings without regard for anyone else. Ideally this would be a private place on a lake, ocean shore, or mountain ridge where you can be alone without concern that anyone will disturb or intrude upon you. If this isn't available, find a time when you can be alone in your house. When you find your place, gather up some rocks to be used as your releasing vehicles. Have one rock available for each sutra. (If you do not have access to open space, find some substitute for the rocks that you can throw without causing damage. Bean bags, water balloons, or tennis balls can work in various settings.)

The power of the releasing ritual is an expression of your attention and intention. Bring the first sutra into your awareness, and hold a rock to your heart. Close your eyes, and, using the sutra as the portal, allow yourself to recall all the painful experiences you associate with the sutra. Envision that the emotional pain you've been carrying is being transferred to the rock you are holding to your heart. Allow your feelings to rise to the surface without resistance. When you feel the rock is fully "charged," throw it into the lake or ocean, or heave it off the ridge with enthusiasm and a shout. Scream, shriek, or curse as you release the painful emotions from your body and your life.

Repeat this process for each sutra. Take your time without rushing the experience. Allow your subconscious mind to bring information into your awareness that carries an emotional charge you would like to discharge. As you proceed with this ritual, strong feelings will rise to the surface. You may experience sadness, grief, anger, or remorse. Whatever comes up, allow it to move through you without judgment. If you perform this exercise with a sense of innocence and openness, you will feel as if space has been freed up in your heart and soul. Although immediately after the process your body may feel spent, soon thereafter you will feel a sense of relief and vitality.

Replenishment

According to the Ayurvedic model of physical purification, once toxins have been eliminated, the body is ready for nourishing input. Substances and experiences that nurture the body at a fundamental level are known as *rasayanas*. A rasayana improves the quality of the tissues and enhances the integration between cells, organs, and physiological systems. A handful of elite herbal medicines are classified as rasayanas because they seem to have a positive effect on many levels of the body.

In an analogous way, we can benefit from emotional rasayana. As we free our hearts from grievances, resentments, and regrets, we can replenish our hearts, minds, and souls with the nurturing emotions of understanding, forgiveness, compassion, and love. In most situations, it is useful to assume that people who hurt others are not usually trying to cause pain intentionally. Rather, in the pursuit of their own needs and as a result of limited emotional resources, they trample the needs of others. Understanding how other people came to be who they are can help relieve the pain created, resulting in forgiveness.

Consider the people with whom you associate emotional pain and compose a biography of their lives, beginning in early childhood. Reflect on the upbringing these people experienced, based upon what you know about their parents or caregivers. Recall or imagine the messages they received about relationships, communication, and love from the people who raised them. If you do not have much direct knowledge of their early lives, make up a story that makes sense to you. Consider the experiences they had as children and adolescents that shaped their personalities. See how these patterns played out in previous relationships and how they affected their interactions with you. As you come to understand the formative events of their lives, you'll take their behavior toward you less personally. Through a greater recognition of their conditioning, you can replace with compassion the hurt or anger you have been carrying.

It is an important principle to remember that everyone is

doing their best at every moment, even though one's best may cause pain to others or to oneself. Just as you would like to be forgiven for choices you've made in the past that hurt other people, seek the understanding that frees your heart from resentment and bitterness.

Although you may believe that your animosity or hostility toward others hurts them, it causes more damage to your heart than to the other person's. The best payback for a broken heart is to get on with your life and choose to be happy. Making the choice to replace toxic emotions with nourishing ones is a major step toward emotional freedom and spiritual evolution.

Growing Up Your Parents

You are not responsible for your inadequate parents, yet you carry the emotional burden for their failure to help you create a healthy self-image with appropriate boundaries. There is nothing you can do about your past, but you can do something now to heal it. You have enough experiences to know how you would have chosen to be raised if you had responsibility for your own upbringing. Knowing the characteristics of healthy parents means that you can access these qualities within your own awareness.

Consider the messages you would have liked to receive growing up. It's usually not too complicated. Children thrive when they are regularly told and shown they are lovable, adorable, and valuable. Conscious parents are continually reinforcing to their children how beautiful, intelligent, powerful, and precious they are. Unconditional love is the only justifiable experience of innocent children.

In your quiet moments, settle into your heart and imagine loving caregivers expressing their approval and appreciation for you. Consider the proposition that there is no reason why you should not have their unconditional love. You came into this world as an open, innocent being with the natural expectation that you deserved to have your core needs met. The fact that your caregivers may not have been qualified to meet your needs is neither your fault nor your responsibility. Therefore, in support of your personal healing and transformation, do not take it personally.

We find it helpful to heed the words of the Sufi poet Hafiz who so eloquently said:

> *Perhaps*
> *For just one minute out of the day,*
> *It may be of value to torture yourself*
> *With thoughts like,*
> *"I should be doing*
> *A hell of a lot more with my life than I am—*
> *Cause I'm so damned talented."*
> *But remember,*
> *For just one minute out of the day.*
> *With the rest of your time,*
> *It would be best*
> *To try*

Looking upon your self more as God does.
For He knows
Your true royal nature.
God is never confused
And can see Only Himself in you.[1]

Reconditioning

Our emotional lives derive from conversations we've internalized. If your inner dialogue has not been generating sensations of peace and happiness, it is time to change the tape. You are the co-creator of your life, and despite what has transpired up until this time, you have the power and creativity to write a new chapter. We encourage you to envision the state of emotional freedom that is your birthright and align your choices with the vision you deserve to manifest.

Conclusion

Escaping the Prison

Understanding the toll addiction takes on people's lives, we wish we could wave a magic wand and effortlessly replace your life-damaging habits with life-nurturing ones. For better or worse, the door to change opens from the inside. The Sufi poet Rumi expressed it best when he said:

> I have lived on the lip of insanity, wanting to know reasons, knocking on the door.
> It opens.
> I've been knocking from inside![1]

Perhaps the most important question to ask yourself when considering giving up something is, "What are the rewards?" Although you may have been conditioned to believe that evading punishment is a sufficient motivator, we disagree. Although avoiding lung cancer, cirrhosis of the liver, or HIV infection are desirable outcomes, we have not written this book to merely help you avoid pain. We understand the longing of your heart and soul to be liberated from the constricted prison of your love-starved existence. We identify with your yearning for freedom and ecstasy. We recognize your hunger for unconditional love, acceptance, and meaning in life. It is because we know that you cannot fulfill these universal needs through a drug or habit that we invite you to choose a different path.

The only effective relief for the existential pain of life is the exhilaration that derives from connection to your own spirit. This inner peace that passes understanding is not flashy or dramatic. It is quiet, comforting, and encouraging. The quest for peace and ecstasy is a path that each of us walks, whether we identify ourselves as addicts or not. We want tranquility, but not so much that we become bored. We want excitement, but not so much that we become lost in the turbulence. We have a desire for balance and a desire to explore the full range of human experience. We like the directive that encourages us to take everything in moderation, including moderation.

Reviewing the Basics

All that we are arises with our thoughts. To manifest real change, we must translate our thoughts into actions. To help you on your journey, remember these key points:

1. Forgive yourself as you make commitments to heal.
2. Begin a daily practice of silent meditation.
3. Think about your choices in terms of nourishment and toxicity, and consciously minimize the experiences that contribute to the contamination of your body, mind, or soul.
4. Ensure that you receive a variety of nurturing sensory experiences on a daily basis. In addition to healthy food, pay attention to the ingestion of healthy sounds, sensations, sights, and smells.
5. Release from your heart the emotional charge associated with unmet needs from your past. Learn to communicate your needs consciously so you gain confidence that your future can unfold differently from your past.
6. Take care of your physical body through daily routines that enhance flexibility, balance, and strength. Become intimate with your breath.
7. Embark on a lifelong voyage of self-discovery. Take the time to quiet your mind and ask questions of yourself to bring clarity into your life.
8. Envision your life as a journey of expanding awareness. Celebrate the expansion of your inner reference point from ego to spirit.

You Are Not a Thing

Throughout this book we have encouraged you to stop thinking of yourself as a separate, isolated entity, but rather to see yourself as a set of relationships woven from the fabric of the universe. Your sense of individuality derives from the beliefs and molecules you have chosen to call your own. Changing your sense of self requires relinquishing some beliefs and embracing others. One of those beliefs you may need to release is that you can handle your addiction on your own. It is not a sign of weakness to ask for help when you need it. We see it as recognition of our essential interrelatedness and interdependency. It may also be an expression of authenticity. At the end of this book we make our recommendations for finding professional help that can support you on your path to wholeness.

Healthy Modulation

Balanced conscious living requires clear communication between your body, mind, and soul. At times, it may seem that too much is happening in your life and you need to turn down the volume. Other times, you may feel that you are in a place of stagnation and need to boost your enthusiasm. Healthy people have clarity regarding their boundaries for acceptable fluctuations in mood and energy, and they adjust their behaviors to stay within those healthy limits. Drugs or addictive behaviors that suppress or stimulate may provide temporary modulation but fail to contribute to authentic or lasting balance. You can learn the skills to be comfortable and feel alive without chemical manipulation, but doing so requires practice. Start with one shift to substitute something nourishing for something toxic and observe the effect. Simplification can catalyze healing. Look at what you can release to create the space your soul can use for evolutionary transformation.

We've shared with you the tools we find to be powerful allies in our universal quest for freedom. Please start using them to build a life full of vitality, love, and meaning. Regardless of what you've been told up until now, you deserve happiness and peace.

Appendix A

Surveying the Landscape

The lure of mind-altering substances has been with us a long time, and there is convincing evidence that even nonhuman animals seek out fermented fruits and psychoactive plants. African elephants travel long distances to imbibe the natural wine of Marula tree fruits, while Amazonian jaguars have been observed chewing on hallucinogenic ayahuasca vines. There are numerous reports of young chimpanzees raiding banana beer breweries in Uganda, becoming intoxicated, and behaving badly.

Among humans, the development of agriculture provided consistent supplies of sugar-containing crops, which, along with the advent of pottery, enabled the reliable production of fermented beverages. Jars with chemical residues of primitive wine have been discovered at Neolithic sites in northern Iran from 7,000 years ago. Egyptians, Mesopotamians, and Babylonians had thriving wine and beer operations over five millennia ago. There is evidence that even then some people had difficulty controlling their consumption, resulting in the first laws regulating intoxicants.

People around the world have ingested psychoactive substances since the dawn of humanity. From the use of marijuana in China over 4,000 years ago to the chewing of coca leaves by the Incas in the thirteenth century, cultures have often authorized the use of botanical agents to alter consciousness.

In most traditions, mind-altering drugs were consumed in the context of medicinal or spiritual ceremonies. Contextualizing psychoactive substances through rituals provided a sanctioned way for people to change their consciousness. Visions resulting from hallucinogenic mushrooms consumed by the seers of ancient India were translated into the hymns of the Vedas. The use of peyote cactus as a religious sacrament by Native American church members has its roots in the tribal rituals of pre-Columbian Mexico. Wine has long been used as a vehicle to connect with the Divine. In ancient Greece, drinking alcoholic beverages invoked Dionysus, the god of ecstasy and excess. All major Jewish holidays incorporate wine, signifying joy and abundance, while in Holy Communion, wine represents a sharing of divinity with humanity.

With the rise of Western civilization, religious uses of psychoactive plants were discouraged and ultimately illegitimatized. Taken out of a cultural and spiritual context, consciousness-altering drugs have a greater propensity for misuse and abuse. In the absence of wise elders, new users have little guidance on how to manage and integrate the potent neurophysiologic shifts that drugs can induce.

Technology has enabled us to extract and concentrate the active ingredients in psychoactive plants, increasing the ease and likelihood of abuse. A farm worker chewing coca leaves to improve endurance in the mountains of Peru rarely develops health-damaging effects, unlike the American businessman who snorts lines of cocaine in order to work late into the night. A Navajo Native American smoking sacred tobacco in a peace pipe would not have imagined that one day millions of people would be inhaling 200-plus doses of nicotine per day through neatly wrapped white cylinders. In our quest to identify and concentrate the active ingredients of nature, we have extracted the intelligence, leaving the wisdom behind.

Modulating from Without

Drugs serve a purpose. When people seek a shift in their emotional states and do not know how to create the change from within, they reach for something outside. Psychoactive chemicals can change one's mood or emotion, but only temporarily. When the drug is gone, the discontent, discomfort, or distress is often worse than before. Then the user must choose to either seek another, more lasting shift or reengage in another short-term dose of relief.

Alcohol and drugs consume tremendous resources. Used judiciously, they can add unique flavors to life, but misused they wreak havoc on individuals, families, and communities. Statistics almost certainly underestimate the number of people whose lives are affected by chemicals with potentially harmful consequences. A brief survey of the most common drugs consumed in the West and their potential and known consequences is offered. It is not intended to be exhaustive, but rather provide a broad overview on the drug culture.

Tobacco

Statistics suggest that almost 30 percent of the U.S. population smoke cigarettes, amounting to over 70 million Americans addicted to nicotine. This includes over 3.5 million young smokers between the ages of twelve and seventeen. Tobacco is responsible for almost 450,000 heart- and lung-related deaths per year and close to $100 billion in direct medical costs. Although legislation and recent lawsuits have had a substantial economic impact, the tobacco industry continues to be a major financial force in the global economy. The combined market value of the two largest cigarette producers, Phillip Morris and RJ Reynolds, is over $160 billion.

Tobacco is a significant revenue generator for governments, through state and federal excise taxes. Excise tax on cigarettes ranges from five cents per pack in North Carolina to $2.46 per pack in Rhode Island, and averages about eighty-five cents across the states. The federal excise tax is currently at thirty-nine cents per pack. Although smokers may decry the nearly $1.25 tax per pack, the U.S. Centers for Disease Control and Prevention estimates that smoking-related health costs amount to over $7 per pack.

Tobacco farming extracts a toll on our environment. The curing of tobacco leaves results in the worldwide deforestation of nearly 500,000 acres each year. Over 25 million pounds of pesticides are used on tobacco crops in the United States, posing health risks to farm workers and surrounding communities. Despite the toxic effects on individuals and the environment, the federal government spent more than $500 million over the past five years subsidizing tobacco production.

Why People Smoke

Smoking fulfills people's needs. The original cigarette experience often represents a declaration of independence from parental authority. It serves as a bonding ritual with other smokers and as a time-out from the pressures of life. Smoking a cigarette or cigar fulfills oral needs. And, after a short induction period, nicotine short-circuits pleasure sites in the brain by mimicking the natural chemical acetylcholine. However, the more one smokes, the less sensitive the brain becomes to internally generated neurochemicals, creating a dependency of the smoker upon regular doses of nicotine from tobacco.

Alcohol

An estimated 15 million Americans have a problem with alcohol, and over one in thirteen adult Americans are alcoholics.

In addition to contributing to significant health, relationship, and work-related problems, about 20,000 deaths each year are directly attributable to drinking, excluding accidents and murders. Overall, 20 percent of fatal auto accidents are associated with alcohol; the number rises to 50 percent when the driver is between twenty-one and forty-four years of age.

Approximately $110 billion is spent each year on alcoholic products in the United States, while the annual medical costs associated with drinking are estimated to be in excess of $185 billion. Since alcohol affects nearly every system in the body, the medical consequences of excessive drinking are widespread. The digestive system is particularly vulnerable, with inflammations of the stomach, liver, and pancreas most common. Some evidence of liver scarring (alcohol cirrhosis) is found in almost 18 percent of daily heavy drinkers. Chronic alcohol consumption is toxic to the nervous system, affecting memory, thinking, and the peripheral nerves. The hormonal, hematological, and reproductive systems also pay a toll for excessive alcohol consumption.

Although light-to-moderate wine drinking (up to six glasses per week) may have a protective effect on the heart due to the presence of natural antioxidants in grapes, excessive alcohol is toxic to the heart muscle.

Why People Drink

In low doses, alcohol sedates, relaxes, and releases inhibitions, serving as a social lubricant. It has a short-term anti-anxiety effect, although it predisposes the drinker to depression with chronic use.

Alcohol acts on the brain by interacting with a neurochemical called GABA. This is an inhibitory molecule that sedates nerve cells. When alcohol is metabolized, the brain becomes more excitable, resulting in anxiety and insomnia.

Stimulants

Considering American culture's attraction to relentless activity, it is not surprising that over 3.5 million Americans use cocaine and over a half million use amphetamines regularly. A study by the U.S. Department of Health and Human Services found that over 12 million people admitted to using methamphetamine at least once in their lifetimes. Mimicking the actions of adrenaline, stimulants can increase heart and blood pressure. They are commonly associated with strokes in young people and with epileptic seizures.

Methamphetamine is relatively easy to make from the over-the-counter decongestant drugs ephedrine and pseudoephedrine, resulting in a proliferation of clandestine labs. The Drug Enforcement Agency (DEA) estimates that over 7,700 of these small-production operations exist in the United States. In addition to the noxious effects on people's nervous systems, amphetamines have a toxic effect on our environment. A number of common but powerful chemicals are used in the preparation of methamphetamines, including drain cleaner, toluene, ether, lithium, and red phosphorus. Laboratory operators routinely dump their waste products in sewage systems, rivers, and streams. The cost to decontaminate a single methamphetamine lab can run between $5,000 and $100,000.

Cocaine delivers a swift and intense euphoria, making it the drug of choice for those seeking a quick surge in self-esteem and confidence. Snorting it produces a slower high that lasts up to half an hour, while smoking it in the form of crack cocaine provides a quicker, more intense rush lasting five to ten minutes. Unfortunately, the boost departs as quickly as it arrives, leaving the user feeling washed out and craving to be re-energized.

Americans spend a lot of money for this brief energy boost, an amount estimated at over $35 billion per year. The price of cocaine on the streets of America has recently risen to about $170 per gram. Some see this as a positive sign, reflecting the Colombian government's efforts to reduce coca leaf production as a result of a $3 billion aid package from the United States. The latest studies suggest that fewer high school students are experimenting with cocaine now than five years ago, giving some people hope that we are past the peak of consumption.

Why People Use Stimulants

Amphetamines and cocaine lead to increased brain levels of the chemicals noradrenaline, dopamine, and serotonin. As a result a person feels energized, powerful, and euphoric. A sense of confidence and self-assurance enables the stimulant user to engage in social interactions and conversations, whereas without the drug he or she may be inherently shy or insecure.

As the drug effect wears off, the brain is left with depleted levels of these critical neurochemicals, resulting in fatigue and depression. The contrast is distressing and leads to repeated use of the stimulant drug.

Opiates

Archaeological evidence suggests that Neanderthals may have harvested opium poppy over 30,000 years ago. Five millennia ago the Sumerians were cultivating the poppy plant (*Papaver somniferum*) for its white juice, known to relieve pain and induce euphoria. They called it *hul gil,* meaning the plant of joy.

For centuries opium played a central role in the healing systems of Egypt, Greece, Arabia, India, and China. It was the preferred prescription of Simon Januensis, the thirteenth-century physician to Pope Nicholas IV. In the mid-sixteenth century, the Swiss alchemist Paracelsus developed an alcohol derivative of opium, which he termed Laudanum, meaning "worthy of praise."

Morphine was first isolated from opium by a German pharmacist, Wilhelm Sertürner, in the early 1800s. He named it after Morpheus, the god of dreams. By the end of the nineteenth century, the German pharmaceutical company Bayer began marketing a chemically modified morphine as a more potent, non-addicting derivative. Free samples were liberally provided to practicing physicians. It was named after the German word *hero-isch*, meaning hero. The drug was heroin.

It took the next couple of decades to recognize the highly addictive properties of morphine and heroin, leading to the passage of the Harrison Narcotic Act of 1914, which required physicians and pharmacists to keep records of opiate drugs prescribed to patients. Because addiction was not considered a disease, physicians who prescribed narcotics to addicts for the purpose of maintaining their addiction were held to be in violation of the law and were often arrested and imprisoned.

It was not until the 1970s that we learned that these drugs work by binding to receptors in the brain, designed to respond to internally generated opiates called endorphins. The chemicals in nature's botanical pharmacy mimic the chemicals in our inner pharmacy. Problems arise when narcotics are consumed to the point that our inner pharmacy shuts down, and withdrawal symptoms result from being left without internally or externally produced pain relievers.

It is estimated that 1–2 percent of the U.S. population is addicted to some form of a narcotic drug. Prescription drug abuse is a growing problem, with oxycodone (OxyContin) and hydrocodone (Vicodin) leading the pack. The physical, emotional, economic, and legal aspects of opiate abuse and addiction are immense: From AIDS to overdosing, to violent crime, the human pursuit to escape from pain carries consequences.

Why People Use Opiates

The seventeenth-century physician Thomas Sydenham, sometime known as the English Hippocrates, said, "Among the remedies which it has pleased Almighty God to give to man to relieve his sufferings none is so universal and so efficacious as opium." Opiate-derived chemicals directly activate the pleasure receptors of the brain, bypassing all usual methods to achieve comfort. While under the influence of a narcotic drug, the user feels relaxed, safe, and protected from the pain and stress of the world.

When the opiates are metabolized, the body is left without intrinsic or extrinsic pain relievers. Cramping, sweating, diarrhea, sleeplessness, and agitation are common symptoms of opiate withdrawal.

Sedatives

Because life can be anxiety provoking, sufferers and scientists have long sought solutions to calm agitated minds. When barbiturates were first synthesized in the early twentieth century, they were widely prescribed as sedatives, sleeping aids, and antiepileptic medications. It wasn't long after their release these drugs were recognized as having significant addictive potential, resulting in tremors, anxiety, and seizures upon their withdrawal, so alternative medicines were sought. The magical

solution to the treatment of anxiety seemed to have been discovered in the early 1960s with the development of Librium and
Valium by the pharmaceutical company Hoffman-LaRoche. By
the mid-1970s almost 60 million prescriptions for Valium had
been written, mostly for frazzled, middle-class women. It was
made famous by the Rolling Stones' hit song "Mother's Little
Helper."

Unfortunately, it was much easier to develop physical and
psychological dependency to Valium than originally thought,
resulting in millions of people experiencing withdrawal symptoms when their prescriptions ran out. Despite this, it remained
the most widely prescribed drug in the world until the early
1980s.

Valium and its chemical cousins are members of the benzodiazepine class of sedative drugs, which work by turning on
inhibitory neurochemicals in the brain. Generously prescribed
by physicians to treat nervousness and insomnia, these drugs
have largely replaced the more addictive and side-effect-ridden
barbiturates. Other members of the benzodiazepine family
include Ativan (lorazepam), Xanax (alprazolam), Klonopin
(clonazepam), and Restoril (temazepam).

Benzodiazepine dependency is associated with drowsiness,
memory impairment, and slowed motor reflexes. Upon withdrawal rebound insomnia and anxiety are common. Addiction
to alcohol and dependency on benzodiazepines share many
similar features.

Why People Use Sedatives

People tend to use sedatives for the same reasons they use alcohol, although communal sedative use is not a socially sanctioned activity. They are usually prescribed for the short-term relief of anxiety, but because people feel more anxious upon withdrawal of sedatives than they did prior to starting them, dependency is common.

Marijuana

Although a relatively small percentage of people enter drug treatment programs for marijuana usage, psychological dependency is common. It is the most frequently used illegal drug in the United States, with a 2002 study estimating that over 14 million Americans smoke marijuana on at least a monthly basis.

The active ingredient in marijuana, delta 9-tetrahydrocannabinol (THC), was identified in 1964, but it was not until the early 1990s that brain receptors for cannabinoids were identified. It is now known that the brain produces natural THC-like chemicals, which play a role in mood, pain, immune activity, digestive function, appetite, and inflammation.

Marijuana advocates promote it as a relatively safe and mild euphoric drug, with potentially useful medical properties. Detractors point out that marijuana smoke contains more carcinogens than tobacco. It has been associated with chronic pulmonary problems, and long-term use can lead to undesirable personality changes, including the so-called amotivational syndrome, in which people lose their drive for personal accomplishment. Users can also experience dry mouth, disorientation, elevated heart rate, anxiety, and paranoia. A recent study from New Zealand reported that habitual cannabis users are almost ten times more likely to be involved in automobile accidents than non-users.

Why People Smoke Marijuana

Marijuana produces a rapid shift in perspective, characterized as emotional detachment from past or future concerns, and heightened sensory perception. Familiar experiences are perceived as novel. Relaxation, pain relief, and reduced social inhibitions are experienced over the first one to four hours after smoking marijuana. Anxiety and depression can occur upon discontinuation, along with lingering impairment in learning and memory.

The medical use of marijuana continues to be a hotly debated topic. Scientific studies have demonstrated its value in treating spasticity in multiple sclerosis and in reducing certain types of chronic nerve pain. It has also been suggested to increase the appetite in patients undergoing chemotherapy for cancer. Society's ambivalence toward recreational drugs with possible therapeutic value is highlighted by the fact that medical marijuana is currently legal in California but illegal in the rest of the United States.

Hallucinogens

Natural substances with mind-altering properties have been known for thousands of years. The pre-Columbian use by Native Americans of peyote cacti, psilocybin mushrooms, and ayahuasca in native ceremonial rituals is well documented. The alphabet soup of synthesized hallucinogenic drugs—LSD, DMT, MDA—have complex neurophysiologic effects, acting primarily on serotonin pathways. Under the influence of these psychoactive chemicals, users experience changes in perception, time, space, and sense of self.

This experience is liberating for some and terrifying for others. The aftermath of an intense hallucinogenic trip may range from a philosophical shift in life values to a psychotic break.

Although the drug ecstasy (MDMA: 3-4 methylene-dioxymethamphetamine) is chemically related to mescaline and amphetamine, it does not usually cause sensory distortions or hallucinations at normal dosages. It produces a sensation of euphoria coupled with empathy and sensual heightening. Frequent or high doses can cause amphetamine-like effects, including jaw muscle tightness and teeth grinding. A frequently quoted University of Chicago study found that rats given large intravenous doses of MDMA showed degeneration of serotonin nerve fibers in certain areas of the brain.

Why People Take Hallucinogens

Hallucinogenic substances create profound shifts in perception, which may be interpreted as alternate realities. Positive
experiences reported by psychedelic drug users include feelings
of deep joy, insights into core beliefs, enhanced empathy and
emotional resonance with others, and a sense of unfiltered communion with the sacred. Because the response to these powerful
chemicals is unpredictable, users can also experience intense
panic, depression, and a weakened sense of self during or after
the drug experience.

The Seduction of Drugs

It is not surprising that human beings consume drugs to help
cope with life. Substances that relieve pain, reduce anxiety,
enhance energy, boost confidence, support intimacy, or provide
glimpses of the divine might be attractive to almost anyone at
some time in life.

But there are two major problems with drugs. The first is the
price of the experience. Most chemicals that influence mood act
by mimicking natural messenger molecules in the brain.
Abiding by the law of conservation of energy, when the brain
receives an external chemical, which mimics what it normally
manufactures, it reduces its production. When the drug is no
longer ingested, the brain is left without an inner or outer

source, creating symptoms that are often opposite the effect of the drug. If a substance increases your energy, you are likely to feel exhausted when it wears off. If the drug has a sedative effect, you will likely experience anxiety and agitation when it is cleared from your body. The debt is often equal to or greater than the desired effect.

The second related problem with using drugs to modulate your feelings is that your inner state becomes dependent upon something external. Even if the drug or behavior has minimal side effects, the dependency upon an outer source for inner comfort leaves one feeling vulnerable. As a consequence more of a person's emotional and psychological resources are consumed to ensure a steady supply of the distress-relieving substance, and anxiety arises if the outer source is unavailable.

Our goal in *Freedom from Addiction* has been to demonstrate that your deepest needs for peace, harmony, ecstasy, meaning, and love can be fulfilled through inner exploration and expansion of awareness. If you can generate these experiences internally, you will experience the freedom of knowing yourself as an expression of the sacred and will not have to pay the potentially significant toll that drugs may extract on your body, mind, and soul.

A Brief History of Addiction

The Spanish philosopher and writer George Santayana said, "Those who cannot remember the past are condemned to repeat it." This brief history of addiction has been shaped through thousands of years of experiences. We hope you'll find it illuminating.

We can recognize the archetypal drama of addiction in the millennia-old tales of Dionysus. The Greek god of indulgence, ecstasy, and excess has always provoked ambivalence. Beloved by revelers and disdained by those who cherish self-restraint, Dionysus is the antithesis of Apollo, who stands for sobriety and moderation. As the illegitimate son of King Zeus, Dionysus repeatedly encountered Queen Hera's contempt. Shortly after learning the art of wine cultivation, the handsome Dionysus was struck by Hera with madness. After years of wandering deliriously around the Earth, he was eventually restored to health by Cybelle, who shared her sacred healing rituals with him.

Dionysus reminds us that we are simultaneously attracted to, and fearful of, the disinhibition caused by intoxication. The desire to engage in behaviors or chemicals to escape from the mundane collides with the potential destructiveness they bring. Throughout the course of humanity, societies have struggled to manage these conflicting impulses.

We can go back through antiquity and hear the warnings about the risks of overindulgence. In Homer's *Odyssey*, we learn of Elpenor, Ulysses' inebriated companion who falls off a roof and fatally breaks his neck. In Proverbs King Solomon tells us that "those who linger long at the wine . . . will see strange things and . . . utter strange things. He who drinks will think—*They have struck me, but I was not hurt. They have beaten me, but I did not feel it. When shall I awake, that I may seek another drink?*" Plato encouraged alcohol abstinence in the young but supported drinking in the elderly (those over forty) as a means to recapture one's youth. Plato promoted sobriety in those seeking to procreate, believing that alcohol led to inferior reproductive tissue.

Wine and beer were the most common beverages consumed throughout the Middle Ages, for sources of water were often contaminated. Known as *aqua vitae*, the water of life, alcohol offered a dependable source of calories and fluids. As Christianity spread through Europe, the church displayed ambivalence toward alcohol. Although indulgence that led to loss of inhibitions was judged to be the remnants of pagan influences, wine was a nearly universal component of religious life. Many monasteries were renowned for their productive vineyards, as wine became the symbol of Christ's blood.

Alcohol, Drugs, and Civilization

Although occasional warnings were raised about the potential harm caused by intemperate drinking, it wasn't until the late 1700s that physicians and politicians in Europe and the New World began addressing alcohol's health and social consequences. English doctor Tomas Trotter suggested that drinking was a weakness of will, while in America, the physician Benjamin Rush declared that the habitual use of alcohol was a serious illness that required treatment.

Rush suggested that for some, alcohol was a form of gradual suicide, while for others it was a type of self-medication providing relief from the overwhelming stresses of life. Aware of the difficulties in treating this disease, Rush advocated the establishment of Sober Houses, specifically dedicated to the care of people addicted to alcohol.

On the other side of the world, opium was becoming the addiction of choice for both individuals and nations. By 1750 the British East India Company had assumed total control over opium production in India and within two decades was shipping over 2,000 chests of opium each year to China. By 1799 Chinese emperor Kia King issued a total ban on opium, making all cultivation and trading of poppies illegal.

This didn't dissuade the British merchants from smuggling opium into Canton to supply the estimated 2 million Chinese addicts. In response to China's attempts to crack down on opium importation, the British government mobilized its naval forces, imposing a blockade on Canton and invading the Chinese coast. From 1839 to 1860 England and China engaged in a series of battles, which came to be known as the Opium Wars. Imperial Britain's military superiority eventually led to the imposition on China of a trade agreement, which included the legalization of opium.

In the last part of the 1800s, China became the primary opium producer for the world. By the turn of the century there were an estimated 13.5 million opium addicts in China and over 300,000 in the United States. By 1907 the United States was importing almost 300 tons of opium each year, and average American consumption increased more than fourfold from 12 grains per person in the 1840s to over 50 grains in 1900.

By the turn of the nineteenth century, societal momentum was building to address the economic, social, psychological, and medical consequences of drugs and alcohol. It was recognized that while individuals have addictions, families and communities shared the pain, and without societal help and support, most people were unable to break their life-damaging habits.

Early Addiction Treatment in America

Public intoxication became increasingly visible during the late 1700s and early 1800s. Original efforts to tackle the problem focused on moderation, giving birth to a number of temperance organizations that believed heavy alcohol users could establish some control over their drinking without having to abstain. It was believed that the gravest health and social risks were with distilled spirits, while the harmful effects of beer and wine were less serious. Drinkers of whiskey, gin, and rum were encouraged to substitute wine, ale, and cider for their hard liquor. It soon became apparent that this was rarely a successful approach, and by the mid-1800s an all-or-nothing strategy, that is, complete abstinence, was seen as the only effective means to control the problem of alcoholic intoxication.

The recognition that sobriety without social support was a difficult path gave birth to numerous community-based approaches. One of the first and most influential was the Washingtonian Total Abstinence Society. Founded in 1840 by six drinking cronies in a tavern in Baltimore, Maryland, the Washingtonian Society required its members to take a pledge of total abstinence and pay monthly dues of twelve-and-a-half cents. Fueled by the emotional stories of lives that had been decimated by alcohol and then resurrected upon enrolling in the organization, the Washingtonian Society established chapters in cities throughout the country.

Energized by charismatic leaders, the Washingtonians claimed 600,000 members at their peak. Significantly, they denied a role for organized religion in the recovery process, believing that camaraderie and community could catalyze the transformation required to overcome addiction. Despite the enthusiasm it originally generated, the Washingtonian movement was unsustainable. Within a decade, almost all of its chapters had disbanded. Although short-lived, it established the template for future community-based recovery organizations.

The first residential treatment centers also came into being during the latter part of the nineteenth century. Inebriate homes and asylums arose in response to the inadequate care for alcoholism and drug addictions that was generally available in psychiatric asylums, where the prescribing of alcohol and narcotics to control behavior was a common practice. A variety of treatment models emerged, including privately run retreat centers, religiously based recovery homes, and state-sponsored institutions.

A number of significant issues in the treatment of addiction emerged during the nineteenth century. Theories about why people become addicted fell into two major camps—those who believed addiction resulted from a deficiency of character or moral will, and those who believed it represented an illness. In modern times we see the same controversy played out in the question, "Is addiction a moral/spiritual issue, or is it a neuro-chemical/biological problem?" A related issue was whether the tendency to become addicted was inherited or acquired. The relative proportion of innate versus environmental factors was, and continues to be, debated.

Was it appropriate to impose rehabilitation on an addicted person? Then as now, this question had ramifications on the role of the legal system in the treatment of addiction. Those who viewed addiction as a vice or sin encouraged the imposition of legal intervention, while those who envisioned it as an illness saw no value in criminalizing addictive behavior.

The most appropriate staff to work in the addiction field was another hot topic of debate a century ago. Some strongly advocated for a workforce of people in recovery, while others believed that only trained professionals could effectively guide people into sobriety.

Could one be cured of the compulsion to engage in an addictive behavior, or was it a chronic condition requiring lifelong management? Although most people in the field concluded that for the addict, any momentary lapse could reignite the previous pattern of indulgence, the concept of harm reduction was introduced. These different points of view were tested in a variety of models and settings throughout the nineteenth and twentieth centuries.

Twentieth-Century Addiction Treatment Approaches

The twentieth century spawned a host of approaches that aimed to control or treat addictive behavior. Those who saw alcoholism as a weakness of will or character established settings designed to rearrange an individual's internal world. The basic premise of these approaches was that if you could withdraw people from the environment that reinforced the undesirable behavior and place them in one that supported desirable habits, the individual would be able to cast off old patterns in exchange for new ones. The separation of alcoholics from society was also promoted as protective to the community.

The legal and medical systems of early twentieth-century America were ill-prepared to handle the increasing numbers of people arrested for public intoxication. Alcoholics frequently moved through the revolving doors between local police stations and hospital detox units. As it became apparent that this approach did not lead to sustained sobriety, local and state psychiatric hospitals were engaged. It was not uncommon for alcoholics to be legally committed for extended stays of more than a year at a time.

As institutions became filled with people facing addictions, various physical, psychological, and pharmacological approaches were tested. Nutritional therapies, exercise classes, work programs, and water therapy were common interventions.

Morphine, chloral hydrate, and atropine were used to treat alcohol addiction. Cocaine was used to treat addiction to morphine. As convulsive therapies and surgical lobotomies gained standing in the treatment of psychiatric illness, they were applied to recalcitrant addiction cases with generally poor results.

Psychoanalytic treatment for addiction gained advocates during the first half of the twentieth century. Psychiatrist Karl Menninger, founder of the Menninger Clinic, is commonly quoted as saying, "Alcohol addiction can be thought of not as a disease, but as a suicidal flight from disease, a disastrous attempt at the self-cure of an unseen inner conflict." Psychoanalytic efforts were directed toward getting patients to understand and resolve their internal conflicts around sexual identity and poor parenting that gave rise to the drinking impulse. Rather than the cessation of drinking, the psychoanalytic approach set the goal as the resolution of neurosis-generating conflicts. As it turned out, psychoanalysis was more effective in theory than practice. While there may be some truth to the contention that alcohol is a symbolic substitute for mother's milk, serving to numb the pain of unresolved childhood conflicts, a purely psychoanalytic approach did not show consistent efficacy in the treatment of alcoholism or drug addiction.

Other psychological approaches for the treatment of addiction were introduced. Counseling methods that treated the family recognized the influence of upbringing on addiction and the role of addiction on family dynamics. Hypnotherapy sessions attempted to replace the deep psychological drives to abuse drugs or alcohol with life-affirming subconscious suggestions. Group therapy sessions that encouraged people to share their personal sagas and provided support to others became standard components of most rehabilitation programs. Behavioral approaches were applied, including aversion therapies in which the undesirable habit was paired with substances that evoked nausea, revulsion, or pain in efforts to condition a person to associate drinking with discomfort and thereby end the habit.

Proponents of these approaches usually claimed initial dramatic success, but over time, the original zeal for a particular intervention waned. The field, however, shifted substantially when political forces, frustrated with the slow and imperfect success of existing programs, imposed legal solutions onto the addiction world.

Alcohol, Drugs, and the Law

Although evidence for the injurious effects of alcoholism was more obvious than that for narcotic abuse, the first major legislative action to regulate intoxicants in America was the Harrison Narcotic Act of 1914. Passed as a law to require narcotic registration, drug enforcement agencies quickly used it to stop any attempt by physicians to treat addicts with narcotics. As a consequence, tens of thousands of people were forced to take their habit underground, feeding an international drug-trafficking network. Although legislation to tighten enforcement was passed a few years later, there was limited evidence that a legal approach was successful. August Vollmer, chief of police in Berkeley, California, expressed his frustration with this tactic in 1936, saying, "Stringent laws, spectacular police drives, vigorous prosecution, and imprisonment of addicts and peddlers have proved not only useless and enormously expensive as means of correcting this evil, but they are also unjustifiably and unbelievably cruel in their application to the unfortunate drug victims. Repression has driven this vice underground and produced the narcotic smugglers and supply agents, who have grown wealthy out of this evil practice and who, by devious methods, have stimulated traffic in drugs."

The lack of success in legislating narcotics away did not deter the passage of the Eighteenth Amendment to the U.S. Constitution, prohibiting the manufacture, sale, and transportation of intoxicating liquors beginning in January 1920.

With their roots in temperance groups from a century earlier, prohibitionists mobilized a massive campaign to free Americans from "the great anaconda, which wraps its coils around home altars to cripple them, to make room for Bacchus." The political pressure to extinguish alcohol drove it underground, just as America was enjoying an economic revival following the end of the First World War.

Speakeasies opened faster than saloons were closed. By the middle of the Roaring Twenties, an estimated 100,000 illegal alcohol clubs flourished in New York City alone. This under-ground economy brought wealth to organized crime families in cities around the country, while fostering corruption at many levels of the political system.

After thirteen years of Prohibition, it became apparent that the "noble experiment" was a failure. Prohibition was unable to fulfill its promise of eliminating undesirable behavior, and in fact had the opposite effect. After a brief initial drop, per-capita alcohol consumption increased during the 1920s. Criminal behavior escalated, and the number of people imprisoned increased dramatically despite substantial increases in law enforcement expenditures. Franklin Delano Roosevelt was elected president in 1932, largely on an anti-Prohibition plat-form. A year later, the Twenty-First Amendment was passed, repealing, for the only time in U.S. history, a ratified constitu-tional amendment.

The Modern Era

The decades following the repeal of Prohibition witnessed the birth of two important movements in the management of alco-hol and drug addiction. One was Alcoholics Anonymous (A.A.). The other was the medical model of addiction treatment.

Alcoholics Anonymous was officially founded in 1935 by Bill Wilson and Dr. Bob Smith, both veterans of numerous sobriety programs. After a spiritual experience in which he literally "saw the light," Bill became convinced that Divine presence was an essential component of recovery. Soon after his revelation, Bill met Dr. Bob, a surgeon who habitually required sobering up before performing operations. Together they committed to sobriety and began recruiting other alcoholics into a community of people committed to abstinence. Over the next few years they codified the essential principles of A.A. into what was to become known as the "Big Book." With the publication of the Twelve Steps and the compelling stories of people who had followed them to recovery, A.A. grew exponentially. By the mid-1950s, it claimed over 200,000 members in seventy countries.

Alcoholics Anonymous offered a formula for success that had been previously elusive to other self-help, mutual-aid organizations. It maintained an egalitarian culture, opening A.A. to members regardless of social class or history. The assignment of sponsors to new members personalized the relationship between the organization and new recruits.

The other vital development during this post-Prohibition period was the redefining of alcoholism from a weakness of character to an illness deserving of treatment. This shift from seeing addiction as a moral issue to a medical one meant that addicts were sick and therefore worthy of compassion rather than disdain. Viewing alcoholism and drug addiction as a public health problem generated new efforts to understand their causes and effects. Multidisciplinary treatment models that focused on the physical, emotional, social, and spiritual components of alcoholism emerged during the mid-1900s.

The pharmaceutical industry's drive to develop and expand the use of psychoactive medications saw the application of these drugs to the treatment of addiction. Several classes of sedative and tranquilizing agents were given to people during acute withdrawal and to assist with maintenance. Major tranquilizers such as chlorpromazine (Thorazine) and sedative drugs like meprobamate (Equinil) were helpful in weaning people off alcohol but had their own problems with side effects and the potential for dependency. Despite the habit-forming qualities of the benzodiazepines (Valium, Librium), they were almost universally prescribed in medically supervised detox units.

As psychiatry embraced a medical model, specific diagnostic categories for mental illness became important. and the concept of dual diagnosis (also known as co-morbidity or co-occurring disorders) gained prominence. Although these terms didn't become popular until the 1980s, mental health professionals recognized decades earlier that drug abuse and psychiatric illness often coexisted in the same person and that efforts to treat addiction without addressing the underlying mental illness were unlikely to be successful.

Drugs to Treat Drugs

The search for medications to treat addiction saw the emergence of three chemicals with widely different effects—

Antabuse (disulfram), methadone, and LSD. Antabuse, a derivative of a chemical used to make synthetic rubber, was found to
interfere with the normal metabolism of alcohol, generating a
toxic reaction. The person who drank alcohol while taking
Antabuse experienced headache, nausea, vomiting, flushing,
shortness of breath, weakness, dizziness, blurred vision, confusion, and even death, and for some who could not muster the
will to stop on their own, Antabuse offered the necessary deter-
rence to overcome the temptation to drink.

Methadone was a German discovery that enabled people
addicted to heroin and morphine to substitute a long-acting oral
narcotic, preventing the symptoms of withdrawal without generating a high. Introduced on a large scale during the Nixon
administration in the early 1970s, community-based methadone
treatment centers were designed as much to deter criminal
behavior as to offer a compassionate approach to narcotic addiction. Methadone maintenance treatment was shown to reduce
the mortality of heroin users by two-thirds and to save society
more than four dollars in legal and medical costs for every dol-
lar spent. Then as now, the idea of maintaining people indefi-
nitely on an addictive medication was controversial, even
though data shows that methadone users live more productive
lives with enhanced social functioning.

Lysergic acid diethylamide (LSD) was accidentally synthesized by Swiss chemist Albert Hoffman in 1938. Recognized as
a powerful psychoactive chemical, LSD was first used by mental

health professionals to enhance insight during therapy and was later applied to people with drug and alcohol addictions. Psychiatrists from British Columbia described the beneficial effects of supervised LSD trips in a 1961 paper, which reported that half of people with severe alcoholism were able to completely eliminate or dramatically reduce their drinking over a nine-month follow-up period. As LSD leaked from academic and medical environments to become the foremost counter-culture drug, legal restrictions curtailed most scientific research and therapeutic application in the United States.

Addiction in the Twenty-first Century

The debates continue. Is addiction a weakness of will or a biological illness? Is total abstinence the only acceptable objective, or is harm reduction a legitimate goal? Religious, spiritual, and secular approaches all have enthusiastic proponents, with little long-term scientific data to help us see through the smoke generated by the fervor. A 1997 study randomly assigned over 1,700 people with alcoholism to one of three treatment groups—an A.A.-based Twelve-Step facilitation, cognitive behavioral therapy, or motivational enhancement therapy. A year after completion of the program, all groups showed improvement, with about 80 percent of people abstinent for 80 percent of the days. Thirty-five percent of people who participated in an in-residence program were completely abstinent one year later, while about 20 percent of people participating in an outpatient program were fully abstinent. There were few significant differences between the three approaches, and matching a program to a person's individual issues did not substantially improve results. There was no "placebo" group, so this study could not reliably determine if any approach was better than none.

Although the consequences of drug and alcohol addiction are generally perceived as more serious, the quest for sobriety is analogous to the millions of people seeking to reach their ideal weight. New dietary approaches are promoted with regularity, and while some people may experience initial results for a time, most eventually regain the lost weight, struggling through recurrent phases of accomplishment and relapse.

It is our belief, based upon our experience, that people can change. We have the gift of free will, which enables us to escape our prison of conditioning and express our unique talents in the world. We hope that the approach presented in this book will prove to be helpful. The principles we offer are those we have found beneficial in our own lives. We share them with the sole intention of relieving the suffering of our fellow human beings who seek what we seek—freedom, love, vitality, meaning, and purpose.

Professional Resources

To locate professional help for the treatment of addiction, go to the website of the **Center for Substance Abuse Treatment (CSAT)**, a division of the U.S. Department of Health and Human Services: http://csat.samhsa.gov/ or call 800-662-4357.

For information about programs and services offered by the **Chopra Center for Wellbeing**, visit www.chopra.com/freedom or call 888-424-6772.

Notes

Introduction

1. Huxley, A. *The Doors of Perception*. London, UK: Chatto & Windus Ltd., 1954.

Chapter 1—Envisioning Freedom from Your Addiction

2. Easwaren, E. *The Upanishads*. Tomales, CA: Nilgiri Press, 1987.

Chapter 2—Expanding the Steps to Freedom

1. Alcoholics Anonymous World Service, Inc. *Alcoholics Anonymous: The Story of How Many Thousands of Men and Women Have Recovered from Alcoholism, Fourth Edition*. New York: 2001.
2. Foundation for Inner Peace. *A Course in Miracles*. Mill Valley, CA: Viking Adult, 1996.
3. Ladinsky, D. *I Heard God Laughing*. Walnut Creek, CA: Sufism Reoriented, 1996.
4. Ruiz, D.M. *The Four Agreements*. San Rafael, CA: Amber-Allen, 1997.
5. Kazantzakis, N. *Zorba the Greek*. New York: Scribner, 1952.

Chapter 3—The Power of Silence

1. Keefer, L., and E.B. Blanchard. "A One-Year Follow-Up of Relaxation Response Meditation as a Treatment for Irritable Bowel Syndrome." *Behavior Research and Therapy* 40 (2002):541–46.
2. Astin, J.A. "Mind-Body Therapies for the Management of Pain." *Clinical Journal of Pain* 20 (2004):27–32.

3. Davidson, R.J., J. Kabat-Zinn et al. "Alterations in Brain and Immune Function Produced by Mindfulness Meditation." *Psychosomatic Medicine* 65 (2003):564–70.

4. Barnes, V.A., H.C. Davis et al. "Impact of Meditation on Resting and Ambulatory Blood Pressure and Heart Rate in Youth." *Psychosomatic Medicine* 66 (2004):909–14.

5. Hill, M., R. Weber, and S. Werner. "The Heart-Mind Connection." *Behavioral Healthcare* 26 (2006):30–32.

6. Creamer P., C.C. Singh et al. "Sustained Improvement Produced by Nonpharmacologic Intervention in Fibromyalgia: Results of a Pilot Study." *Arthritis Care Research* 13 (2000):198–204.

7. Ott, M.J., R.L. Norris, and S.M. Bauer-Wu. "Mindfulness Meditation for Oncology Patients: A Discussion and Critical Review." *Integrative Cancer Therapies* 5 (2006):98–108.

8. Lee, S.H, S.C. Ahn et al. "Effectiveness of a Meditation-Based Stress Management Program as an Adjunct to Pharmacotherapy in Patients with Anxiety Disorder." *Journal of Psychosomatic Research* 62 (2007):189–95.

9. Sephton, S.E., P. Salmon et al. "Mindfulness Meditation Alleviates Depressive Symptoms in Women with Fibromyalgia: Results of a Randomized Clinical Trial." *Arthritis and Rheumatology* 57 (2007):77–85.

10. To find a Chopra Center–certified Primordial Sound Meditation teacher, go to www.chopra.com/instructors/.

Chapter 4—Detoxifying Your Body, Mind, and Soul

1. Bloedon, L.T., and E.O. Szapary. "Flaxseed and Cardiovascular Risk." *Nutrition Review* 62 (2004):18–27.

2. Coulman, K.D., Z. Liu et al. "Whole Sesame Seed Is as Rich a Source of Mammalian Lignan Precursors as Whole Flaxseed." *Nutrition and Cancer* 52 (2005):156–65.

3. Naik, G.H., K.I. Priyadarsini et al. "In Vitro Antioxidant Studies

and Free Radical Reactions of Triphala: An Ayurvedic Formulation and Its Constituents." *Phytotherapy Research* 19 (2005):582–86.

4. Sandhya, T., K.M. Lathika et al. "Potential of Traditional Ayurvedic Formulation, Triphala, as a Novel Anticancer Drug." *Cancer Letters* 231 (2006):206–14.

5. Heatley, D.G., K.E. McConnell et al. "Nasal Irrigation for the Alleviation of Sinonasal Symptoms." *Otolaryngology—Head and Neck Surgery* 125 (2001):44–48.

6. Sources for detoxifying Ayurvedic teas, Triphala, and neti pots: Triphala (also spelled trifala) is available at most local health food markets, as are neti pots in a variety of shapes and materials. You can also find these detoxifying aids on the Chopra Center website: http://store.chopra.com/.

Chapter 5—Feeding Your Body, Nourishing Your Mind

1. Vanderark, S.D., and D. Ely. "Biochemical and Galvanic Skin Responses to Music Stimuli by College Students in Biology and Music." *Perceptual and Motor Skills* 74 (1992):1079–90.

2. Hirokawa, E., and H. Ohira. "The Effects of Music Listening After a Stressful Task on Immune Functions, Neuroendocrine Responses, and Emotional States in College Students." *Journal of Music Therapy* 40 (2003):189–211.

3. Suggested music to nurture your body, mind, and soul:
Buddha Café. Various Artists, Intent City, 2001.
Embrace. Deva Premal, White Swan, 2002.
Feet in the Soil. James Asher, New Earth Records, 2002.
A Gift of Love: I and II. Deepak and Friends, Rasa Music, 1998, 2002.
Magic of Healing Music. Bruce and Brian Becvar, Shining Star, 1998.
Relax 2: Sublime Music for Reading and Lounging, Various Artists, Rasa Music, 2004.

The Soul of Healing Meditations. Deepak Chopra, Rasa Music, 2001.

4. Field T.M., S.M. Schanberg et al. "Tactile/Kinesthetic Stimulation Effects on Preterm Neonates." *Pediatrics* 77 (1986):654–58.

5. Billhult A., I. Bergbom, and E. Stener-Victorin "Massage Relieves Nausea in Women with Breast Cancer Who Are Undergoing Chemotherapy." *Journal of Alternative and Complementary Medicine* 13 (2007):53–58.

6. Ironson, G., T. Fields et al. "Massage Therapy Is Associated with Enhancement of the Immune System's Cytotoxic Capacity." *International Journal of Neuroscience (*1996): 84:205–17.

7. Perlman A.I., A. Sabina et al. "Massage Therapy for Osteoarthritis of the Knee." *Archives of Internal Medicine* 166 (2006): 2533–38.

8. McClelland, D.C. "The Effect of Motivational Arousal Through Films on Salivary Immunoglobulin A." *Psycholology and Health* 2 (1988):31–52.

9. Kumari, T., R. Fujiwara et al. "Effects of Citrus Fragrance on Immune Function and Depressive States." *Neuro-immunomodulation* 2 (1995):174–80.

10. Edris A.E. "Pharmaceutical and Therapeutic Potential of Essential Oils and Their Individual Volatile Constituents: A Review." *Phytotherapy Research* (2007).

11. Shibata H., R. Fujiwara et al. "Restoration of Immune Function by Olfactory Stimulation with Fragrance." In Schmoll, H., U. Tewes, and N.P. Plotnikoff, eds., *Psychoneuroimmunology.* Lewiston, NY: Hogrefe & Huber Publishers, 1992, 161–71.

Chapter 7—Emotional Emancipation

1. Ladinsky, D. *The Subject Tonight Is Love: Sixty Wild and Sweet Poems of Hafiz.* New York: Viking Penguin, 2003.

Conclusion—Escaping the Prison

1. Barks, C., and M. Greene *The Illuminated Rumi.* New York: Broadway Books, 1997.

Index